You Say You Want A REVOLUTION?

40 DAYS IN THE GOSPEL OF LUKE

DAN BOONE

THE FOUNDRY
PUBLISHING

Cover designer: J.R. Caines
Interior designer: Sharon Page

Note on the cover design: Tradition has it that the winged bull symbolizes Luke and his Gospel as a representation of service, sacrifice, and strength.

Library of Congress Cataloging-in-Publication Data
Names: Boone, Dan, 1952- author.
Title: You say you want a revolution? : 40 days in the gospel of Luke / Dan Boone.
Description: Kansas City, MO : Beacon Hill Press of Kansas City, [2018] |
    Includes bibliographical references.
Identifiers: LCCN 2017044851 | ISBN 9780834136755 (pbk.)
Subjects: LCSH: Bible. Luke—Devotional literature. | Jesus Christ—Meditations.
Classification: LCC BS2595.54 .B66 2018 | DDC 226.4/06—dc23 LC record available at https://
lccn.loc.gov/2017044851

The internet addresses, email addresses, and phone numbers in this book are accurate at the time of publication. They are provided as a resource. Beacon Hill Press of Kansas City does not endorse them or vouch for their content or permanence.

10 9 8 7 6 5 4 3 2 1

CONTENTS

INTRODUCTION

When you open the Gospel of Luke, you realize immediately that you are in a different neighborhood. The stimulating characters, the fast-moving narrative, the tension between groups, the presence of the outcasts, and the spiral toward a crucifixion make Luke different from the other Gospels. His is also the only Gospel that sets us up for Act II, commonly known as The Acts of the Apostles. Most of the barrier-breaking, boundary-bursting activity of Luke's Gospel continues via the followers of Jesus in the second act.

Maybe the radical difference we note in Luke comes from the thought that Luke himself is an outsider. He begins by addressing Theophilus, a Roman official. Then he rewrites the family tree of Jesus, beginning with Adam rather than with Abraham, in order to connect Jesus to all humans, not just the Jewish ones. But it is obvious that he has many other outsiders in mind: Samaritans, the poor, gentiles of every stripe, powerless women, outcast tax collectors, notorious sinners, soldiers, bleeding women, the ostracized impure, a foot-massaging prostitute, an uninvited banquet guest, party crashers, a complaining widow, Zacchaeus, and a host of other excluded characters who would never be found in the winner's circle.

The ministry of Jesus culminates on a cross of utter rejection. He dies in the same place where the done-with and condemned die. Luke introduces us to a Jesus who makes us uncomfortable. Of course, we have tamed this version of Jesus well in the American church by politicizing Jesus for our security, wealth, and comfort. But Luke is still there, waiting for us to read the story again.

And what we will find, when we do read it again, is the original expression of social justice. Sadly, the idea of social justice has become a political and even religious hot potato. Political agendas have hijacked the term for their own purposes so that, to those on the opposing end of the political spectrum, the term itself leaves a bad taste in the mouth. But long before this recent occurrence, the church was actively engaged in social justice. And it still is. But the founding narrative of biblical social justice has been lost in the mix. This volume on Luke's Gospel is an attempt to revisit the narrative of Luke as a guiding story of social justice for the people of God. In Luke, we see Jesus doing social justice. Then in Acts, we see his disciples following in his footsteps. The time has come for the church to engage social justice again.

HOW TO USE THIS DEVOTIONAL

Commentaries on the Gospel of Luke abound. This is not one of them. Across a life of ministry, I have used commentaries with deep appreciation for the remarkable scholarship brought to bear on the ancient texts. These commentaries have spanned the gamut from complex and historical criticism to social customs of biblical days to theological ideas. Each is helpful for the serious student.

The intent of this work on Luke is to connect the primary meaning of the text to the world we encounter today. I have not covered every text but have focused on the primary narratives. And, though I think the Gospel of Luke speaks most acutely to the issue of social justice in our world, I have intentionally sought not to hamstring each text with a social justice implication. Some texts speak more directly to the insiders than to the outsiders.

This devotional has four sections on each text covered.

The Big Idea offers a theological statement or summary description of the issue addressed in the text. It gives context for and explains the tone of the text.

Core Teachings examines and explains key sections of the text, with an emphasis on what we can learn about Jesus and how we can follow more faithfully.

Going Deeper looks at the themes and, by using examples and illustrations, explores what it means to live out our faith daily.

Consider This is comprised of discussion questions for individual or group study and suggestions for daily practices to make the text come alive.

May the same gracious Spirit who inspired Luke to write be with you as you open yourself to the transforming story of Jesus.

A BIBLICAL BASIS FOR SOCIAL JUSTICE

Given the fuzziness that often exists around the term *social justice*, I thought I'd take a stab at explaining what Christians mean when we use these words. Our definition comes from a specific theological viewpoint that is rooted in the Bible. So, if you're up for a little excursion through the primary themes of our Christian Scriptures, come along. Thankfully, there are multiple places where we can lay a foundation for biblical social justice in solid concrete.

1. Creation Theology. Here we find restoration of the earth, humans, human relationships (including marriage), providing food and shelter and clothes, and being good caretakers. All of this rises from a proper understanding of creation. And I don't just mean Genesis 1–2. God, as Creator and Sustainer of the universe, suggests to us that this sphere in which we live is intentionally crafted and sustained by God. Our calling is obedient participation in the character and ways of God. The world is healed when we are good creatures of a good God. The world is fractured when we play God ourselves and raid the tree in the center of the garden. We can look back to Eden for clear teaching regarding God's desire to work alongside us in the garden for the good of the whole creation.

Another significant text for creation theology is Isaiah 40–55. The people of God, living under Babylonian exile, have no future, and the prophet constantly reminds them that their God created the heavens and the earth and that this God is still creating. If they will submit as clay in the Potter's hands, this God will do a new thing. Actually, better than that, this God is already doing a new thing if they can only come into alignment with it.

Such a theology suggests that, as exiled humans living in political and theological systems, we should be embracing our Creator God to see the new thing he is doing. Political, military, and economic systems are not the final word. As God worked his future through the pagan Cyrus, who did not even know God, this same God is at work redeeming all of creation even now (Isaiah 45–46). Creation theology ought to keep us saying, "This is not how God intended it to be, and God has not folded his tent and gone home."

2. Another theological foundation for social justice is a healthy **eschatology**: a sense of how things will come to an end—which, for us, is actually a new beginning. I believe that much of the grief Christians take over social justice from well-meaning brothers and sisters is a result of some Christians having no biblical eschatology, or theology of the future. If I believe that judgment is coming, that the earth will be destroyed by fire, and that the planet will be discarded like a limp rag, then why would I see the need to be a good steward of it? I'll just keep singing, "This world is not my home, I'm just a-passin' through; my treasures are laid up somewhere beyond the blue. The angels beckon me from heaven's open door, and I can't feel at home in this world anymore." This mindset is, essentially, an escapist eschatology. *Let's snag all the souls we can, get them to pray the sinner's prayer, and warehouse them at the bus stop for heaven (usually called 'church'), safe from the evils of this dark world, and keep them there until death comes or Jesus swoops down to* *get them.* I heard this mentality preached for years—and it isn't biblical, but lots of folk believe it is.

So what *is* biblical?

Romans 8: The whole creation groans for its freedom from bondage and decay, and for the return of its Creator who will restore it as the handiwork of God.

Revelation 21: The Holy City is coming down to earth and God announces, "I will make my home among mortals and bring an end to dying and sighing and pain. I will make all things new." I wish N. T. Wright were required reading in every church. His book *Surprised by Hope* will give you a solid place to stand regarding the future.

And what does any of this have to do with social justice? Glad you asked. In the words of Steven Covey, we begin with the end in mind. What will the earth be like the day after Jesus returns? How will humans be treating each other? How will money and power be used? How will governments rule? How will poverty and sickness and trafficking and pollution and rape and war have been dealt with? As Jesus will confront evil then, so do we now. We are the people who have the deposit of the Holy Spirit given to us as a down payment of what the future will look like (Ephesians 1:13–14). God is coming here. The movement of God is not to take us away from here, to some other place, but to reign among us.

3. Shalom. Walter Brueggemann writes about this rich biblical theme with depth and vigor. The word means peace, well-being. This Old Testament idea of the blessing of God is a central biblical theme: our enjoyment of the gift of life. This blessing is what God intended to offer to all the nations of the world through the obedience of his people, Israel, and then through his Son and the body of Christ, the church. Our primary calling is not to get saved but to be the saved bearers of the good news of shalom to all peoples. We are saved into an agenda of peace-making in the world. Peace/shalom is what we wish for all humans, all families, all cities, all lands, all nations—and we are called to bring peace wherever we can.

4. Justice. John Howard Yoder, in *The Politics of Jesus,* exegetes the Hebrew word *misphat,* or righteousness. Righteousness is another significant theme. If *holy* means that God is different, in a category alone and above all, then *justice* is how this holy God engages the world and makes things right. We participate in the right-making work of God in the world. The heart of biblical justice is to make things right according to the character and command of the Father in heaven. The Lord's Prayer is a petition for justice: "thy kingdom come, thy will be done on earth, as it is in heaven" (Matthew 6:10, KJV).

5. And holding hands with justice is **biblical love**—holy love. Holy love, as the distinguishing declaration of God, is essential to a Wesleyan understanding of God and the foundation of social justice.

Our Reformed brothers and sisters begin with the sovereignty of God, which sounds very much like the kingdom of God language that I'll be using before we're done. Sovereignty is about power and authority—the ability to make happen what you want to make happen. This kind of thinking has lots of illustrations: the religious right, where we take back our country by the power of the vote; the KKK, where we intimidate people into conforming to our understanding of the world; the radical Jihadists, where we fight for God by killing infidels. Hear me carefully: our Reformed friends are not Jihadists or the KKK or the religious right. But when you begin your theology with the sovereignty of God and make it about power, you will soon find yourself debating the authority of the Bible, right doctrine, and proper orthodoxy as the human expression of this God.

Wesleyans, on the other hand, begin with the holy love of a God who is so deeply relational that we understand God as a small group: Father, Son, and Spirit. *Covenant* is the name of the relationship. God has emptied himself of his rights as sovereign, taken the form of a servant by being human, and submitted himself to death on a cross. God has not chosen to sovereignly overpower our evil but, rather, to become like us in suffering under it and in it. He has gone, on the cross, into the deepest pit that any human will be found in—because he loves us. The footprints of God are to be found in the gas ovens of Germany, the marches of Alabama, the prisons of South Africa, the chemical victims of Syria. The worst places humans are, God is there in Jesus. And he has gone to the pit of death yielding his life, to be raised by the Creator God to a new beginning. This is our theology: a holy God of suffering love who does not overpower evil but who suffers with us toward the hope and promise of a new creation.

This God offers us inclusion in his life. The Hebrew word for the biding covenant that God establishes with us is *chesed*: what each of us (God and God's covenant partners) have the right to expect of each other in light of the promises that have been made. This covenant love is seen in the Noah story. God regretted in his heart that he even created us and moved via the flood to wipe out all trace of humankind. The flood was God's delete button. When we were one floating zoo from extinction, the text says, "But God remembered Noah" (Genesis 8:1). The flood story is about a God who chose, by means of divine retribution (the flood), not to deal with evil but, instead, offer covenant to Noah and his family. Since that day, God has participated in our suffering rather than cause it. Holy love, covenant love, *just love* is the hallmark of the God we have experienced in our Wesleyan circles of thought.

We are the theological heirs of a man named John Wesley. His theological roots are in the Anglican Church and early Methodism. Wesley experienced God as holy love expelling sin. This love restored him in likeness to Jesus. Wesley saddled a horse and rode into the world with an open Bible on his lap. This is who we are—going out, shaped by the story of God's suffering love, understanding the world through Scripture as we live in the middle of it. We are not hiding in churches or debating doctrines or trying to defend God. We are en route to redeem creation. Wesley saw children in factories who needed education, debtors in prison who needed money, the poor who needed food and shelter, the sick who needed medical care. He preached in coal mines and open fields and town squares. And he raised up an army of Methodists who were unafraid to roll up their sleeves and get to work. He wrote about health, money, estate gifts, economic theory, personal care, literature, politics, science, and the arts. This is why we cannot surrender the political, economic, military, and environmental realms without making the claim that our God has designs on how we go about life. We are in covenant with a God who participates in human suffering as flesh-and-blood followers of the flesh-and-blood Jesus.

6. The kingdom of God. I was confronted by the reality of the kingdom of God in 1972 as a sophomore at Trevecca Nazarene University. One of the most respected Christians on the planet, Dr. E. (Eli) Stanley Jones, spoke in chapel one morning, and more than forty years later, I am still captivated by what he had to say. He was in his eighties and was writing a book on the same topic he spoke on that morning: *The Unshakable Kingdom and the Unchanging Person*. I still have my 1972 edition of that book.

He talked to us about the kingdom of God. The kingdom of God was the primary message of Jesus. Jesus talked more about the kingdom of God than any other topic. What is the kingdom of God? Some say it is heaven, where we will go after we die. Some say it is the ultimate place of safety and refuge that we escape to. Some say it is the church, where people serve God. Some say it is the future that will dawn on us when Jesus returns to earth.

The kingdom of God is a realm, a reality, a sphere, an environment that is filled with the uncontested presence of God. I want to make sure you understand the geography. We are not down here and the kingdom of God way off up there, beyond the last star we can see, in a place that spaceships can't ever get to. We are here, and the kingdom is also here, though we may or may not recognize it. It is not somewhere beyond the clouds but as close as your breath. It is not always visible, but sometimes it does break into the visible realm to make a dramatic difference in what happens. The kingdom of God has come among us in the person of Jesus Christ. He is here, and the kingdom is here in him.

When the disciples asked Jesus to teach them to pray, he said, "Our Father in heaven, hallowed be your name. Your kingdom come, your will be done on earth as it is in [your kingdom]." The kingdom of God exists wherever God's will is being done. And we end up praying this risky, crazy prayer that imagines the world we are living in made right by the in-breaking kingdom. I believe this is the most life-altering, radical, dangerous, consequential prayer we can pray: "Your kingdom come, your will be done on earth."

The kingdom of God intersects with every major and minor that we teach at Trevecca. It is embedded in human tissue, economic theory, political philosophy, interpersonal relationships, power, work, play, entertainment, music, thought, athletics, and health. The kingdom comes to earth in the same way that the kingdom of God came in Jesus: a body. First the body of Jesus of Nazareth, then the body of the resurrected Christ. The body of Christ—that would be all the Christians—exists to receive and live out the kingdom of God in a visible way. When we do God's will on earth, the kingdom has broken through in flesh-and-blood reality. We are kingdom boots on the ground at work in the redemption of all things.

I love to go to Disney World. There is something magical about the place. The "magic kingdom," they call it. Well, it is and it isn't. The kingdom of Disney is created by a particular way of doing things. The territory is defined. You know when you are entering it. It has a look, a feel, a style. Companies have studied the Disney philosophy, trying to replicate it. Everything is intentional. And the people who work there go through discipleship training in Disney-dom. They know exactly what they should and should not do. They are the walking brands of Disney. They are radically obedient to its ways. If you are a Disney employee, much is required of you. There are lots of rules in the place. Disney doesn't just happen. Neither does the kingdom of God. It is a way of living that is embedded in likeness to Jesus, empowered by the Spirit of the risen Jesus. We teach that way of life in our Center for Social Justice.

When we began the J. V. Morsch Center for Social Justice at Trevecca Nazarene University, I fielded questions about the use of *social justice* terminology. Glenn Beck has said that if your preacher says "social justice," go running from your church. Rush Limbaugh has called it "code language for communism." We dealt openly with these questions. I chose to champion a Center for Social Justice in a Christian university because a generation is rising with the hope of joining the right-making work of God. And when they get ready to go to college and prepare to make things right, and they google *social justice*, I want them to see our brand, our program, and our biblical understanding.

I don't spend much energy in the big, populist causes that dominate right- and left-wing TV talk shows—causes that are primarily about getting their people in seats of power. I'd rather be preparing a grassroots army of graduates who will go to all the little places where the footprints of Jesus can be found and empty themselves in skilled, effective, compassionate service. I sense the call of God to lead the kind of university that graduates people like this and, thereby, fills the world with hope. Let's do this work because it is the essence of the story we find ourselves in—the biblical story of the redemption and resurrection of all things.

THE VULNERABILITY OF GOD

SCRIPTURE

Luke 1:26–38

THE BIG IDEA

The incarnation was an act of vulnerability on God's part. This is how God enters into our full humanity and suffers with, for, and in us.

CORE TEACHING

We are vulnerable, and we know it. We have seen high-tech space shuttles disintegrate, leaving no trace of human remains; skyscrapers collapse; stock markets plummet, rearranging retirement plans; companies bought, sold, and moved with city-wrecking swiftness; viruses spread, kill, and mutate; radicals who believe their god has told them to behead us; babies snuffed out in the womb because their timing was inconvenient; the earth poisoned, polluted, and warmed to its destruction; health disappear at the reading of a blood test; careers end with the slip of a tongue; hurricanes ravage life for millions; governments fail to deliver financial responsibility; and nations bring the world to the brink of war.

Any serious person who thinks about the way the world is and seems to be headed has reason to feel vulnerable. And we do all kinds of things to cope with our vulnerability. Some of us numb ourselves to it by way of too much TV, sports, novels, eating, or . . . you can fill in the blanks. Some of us busy ourselves to avoid serious thought about life. Some of us power up and create safe zones, our protected space. We guard our space and wall ourselves in from unwelcome intruders and inconvenient people. We live between fearful avoidance and tough posturing. But we're still vulnerable.

Our own vulnerability is why we love Mary, who is the very picture of vulnerability. Look her up in your pictorial dictionary. How tall is she? How old? Where is she standing? What is she wearing? What color is her hair? How is it fixed?

At the Nelson-Atkins Museum of Art in Kansas City, you can see Mary through the eyes of the artists of the ages. In the composite, she is a mature adult, wears velvet dresses (usually of a deep red), lives in a larger-than-average home, has a chair by the window through which light cascades softly, and she likes to read. This is the Mary of classic art. And she appears to be fully in charge of her space.

But we know better. Mary is in middle school. She wears Walmart or Old Navy clothes at best. She can't read because girls of her day rarely did. Her parents make all the decisions that affect her life, including the one that mandates she be married to an older man named Joseph. We don't know if she even likes him. She lives in a two-bit town without a McDonald's or even a stoplight. And into the humble life of this child comes the brightly beaming, divine messenger whose name means "God has shown himself mighty." She stands there in her flannel nightgown, her hair braided by her best friend, wearing Big Bird house shoes. If you ask me, this is divine overkill.

Defenseless? I think so. Fragile? Yes. Overwhelmed? Most likely. Vulnerable? Definitely.

That's why we adore her. We can get our human arms around Mary. She's like us. She has had overwhelming stuff happen to her. She has faced life with little power to make it turn out the way she planned. Forces beyond herself have rearranged her life. She's the matron saint of the vulnerable.

If you ever think your story is not in the Bible, go see Mary. We're vulnerable, just like her. Mike and Cheryl lost their baby boy within days of a meningitis diagnosis. Julie died of ovarian cancer, leaving two little girls behind. Emily's husband walked out on her two weeks ago. Tyler is in counseling for depression. He's nine. Aaron can't come back to college next semester because his dad lost a job. Foreign relations aren't exactly going the way we had hoped. Health insurance is no longer a benefit. It's an out-of-pocket expense. Tom is failing high school, but he doesn't care. He just plays XBox.

We can get our arms around Mary because she seems to know how we feel. But Mary may not be the most vulnerable one in the story. There is one who becomes even more vulnerable—the God who becomes dependent flesh in the womb of a vulnerable Mary. This story may seem to magnify Mary, but it's really about God—and God's vulnerability.

God, the Creator, becomes creature. God, the breath of every living thing, becomes embryo. God, whose hand scoops out oceans, floats in a fetal sac. God, whose voice splits cedar trees, cries for mother's milk. God, who crushes kings' armies, can't walk. God, who feeds all living things, is hungry. God, who is sovereign, cannot defend himself. God, full of glory, poops and pukes.

On the day that Gabriel came to visit Mary, on the day that the Holy Spirit came upon her, on the day that the power of the Most High overshadowed her, on that day: God became vulnerable. How vulnerable?

Herod hunted him. Hometown folk reached for rocks to stone him. Pharisees criticized him. Family members thought him nuts. A friend turned on him. Liars testified against him. Rulers chickened out on justice and caved in to the demands of a lynch mob. City folk spit on him. Soldiers crucified him. Dying thieves mocked him. Pious leaders taunted him as he died.

That's how vulnerable God became that day in Mary's womb. What happens to us has already happened to God. God came into our vulnerability and met us there.

GOING DEEPER

We tend to prefer Gabriel, messenger of "the God who shows himself mighty." When we are vulnerable, we want to behold a delivering, transforming, world-altering, situation-changing, putting-me-back-in-control kind of God. We ask God to meet us at the intersection of Fixed and Finished.

But God has chosen instead to meet us in the vulnerable Christ, revealing himself at the point of our vulnerability. The saints of the Psalms knew this. It's why they prayed, *I'm afraid. I don't know where to turn. I can't go on much longer. I can't fix this. I'm in a mess of my own making. I've fallen and I can't get up. I'm dying down here. Do you even care?*

Jesus Christ is God's answer to all those prayers. Dare we meet the mighty God at the point of human vulnerability? Browse the Psalms for the cries of vulnerability that were expressed to God. As you pray, focus on all the vulnerable populations of your city and of the world. Is there is a specific ministry of your congregation that serves vulnerable people? Consider interviewing the leaders of this ministry in order to gain a better understanding of the feelings of vulnerability in your community. Then pray with those same leaders.

CONSIDER THIS

1. Describe a time in your life when you felt vulnerable.

2. Put yourself in Mary's shoes. How do you think she felt standing before the mighty angel of God?

3. What danger could there be in thinking about God as vulnerable?

4. How is the characterization of God as vulnerable comforting or disturbing to you?

5. Why do you believe God came this way?

2

YOU SAY YOU WANT A REVOLUTION?

SCRIPTURE

Luke 1:39–80

THE BIG IDEA

"The Magnificat" is one of the classic songs of the theology of Advent. Placed on the lips of a young virgin, it is usually interpreted softly and sweetly—but it is anything but that. It is a song of radical revolution that challenges the power structures of the day.

CORE TEACHING

Songs of revolution abound. The American Civil Rights movement sang "We Shall Overcome." Peter, Paul and Mary sang Vietnam-era songs like "If I Had a Hammer," "Blowin' in the Wind," and "Where Have All the Flowers Gone?" Bob Dylan sang "The Times They Are A-Changin'."

The Broadway production *Les Miserables* gave us "Do You Hear the People Sing?" And the Beatles asked, "You say you want a revolution?" Yet when we list classic songs of political overthrow, civil protest, and revolution, no one ever suggests "The Magnificat," even though Mary's song fits the genre. Some biblical scholars believe the song to be a Maccabean war song. The Maccabees were Jewish nationalists, underground rebels, freedom fighters, and patriots who wanted the occupying enemy out of their country.

Luke is certainly no stranger to the political alignments in his narrative of Jesus's birth. Each birth story begins with some mention of the existing powers. The story of Zechariah (Luke 1) begins with a note about King Herod. The birth of Jesus (Luke 2) begins with a note about Emperor Augustus, Quirinius, and taxation. The story of the ministry of John the Baptist (Luke 3) begins with mention of the reign of Emperor Tiberius, Governor Pontius Pilate, Tetrarchs Herod, Philip, and Lysanius, and High Priests Annas and Caiaphas. I suppose these must all have been rulers who were or may have been threatened by the Messiah.

Mary sang in the past tense—as if the revolution had already occurred. The song is about upheaval of the existing social order, reversal of economic status, and overthrowing of power. Jesus's strategy is all there in miniature in the song. God will show mercy to the lowly, confront the powerful, feed the hungry, send the rich away empty, topple thrones, announce good news to the poor, and keep his promises to Abraham's descendants. When we participate in the way of Jesus, we are radical revolutionaries of the most dangerous kind. We actually intend to crown a new King over all creation.

GOING DEEPER

This stream of thought continues when Mary's song ends. Beginning with Luke 1:67, Zechariah, whose tongue had been loosed, prophesied things like salvation from enemies, a new ruler, mercy, covenant faithfulness, light in the darkness, and a new day of peace. The songs of Advent announced a new world.

Take a copy of your local newspaper or access your favorite source for daily news. How do Mary's and Zechariah's songs run counter to the day's headlines?

Christmas has the tendency to make us sentimental. The coming of God is about a new reign. The people of God are called to radical obedience. We are called to be holy in the same way that our Father in heaven is holy. Discuss how the radical nature of the kingdom infringes on your own self-rule. If the prayers represented by Mary's and Zechariah's songs were instantly answered in your life, how would you be changed?

CONSIDER THIS

1. List the Old Testament themes that appear in the two songs sung by Mary and Zechariah.

2. How would the Gentile world have received these Jewish expressions? How did Luke begin to let non-Jews in on the good news of Jesus?

3. Is Christianity too tame to be real?

4. Rewrite Mary's and Zechariah's songs in your own cultural language.

LAS POSADAS

SCRIPTURE

Luke 2:1–7

THE BIG IDEA

In the classic text for Christmas Eve, we find God—our most hospitable Creator of place and home—seeking a place for the birth of his Son. Will God find the same hospitality that has been offered to us?

CORE TEACHING

Christmas observances in Mexico begin with *Las Posadas*, a nine-day reenactment of Mary and Joseph's search for lodging in Bethlehem. Children gather each afternoon for nine consecutive days leading up to Christmas. One child plays the role of Mary (*la Virgen María*). Another is Joseph (*San José*). Others are the angels (*los angeles*). Still more are the three wise kings (*santo reyes*). And the rest are shepherds (*pastores*). All the children are decked out in colorful, handmade costumes, and they carry paper lanterns (*faroles*). They form the parade of Holy Pilgrims (*Santos Peregrinos*). They go from house to house requesting lodging (*posada*). They sing outside the front door, "*En nombre del Cielo, buenos moradores, dad a estos viajeros posada esta noche* (In the name of heaven, good inhabitants, give these travelers lodging tonight)."

From inside the house comes back the reply, "This is not an inn, move on. I cannot open, lest you be a scoundrel." The children go on singing, explaining that they have traveled from Nazareth, are tired, and that Mary is expecting a child. All to no avail. For eight days they seek shelter and are repeatedly turned away. Finally, on Christmas Eve, they are told that there is no *posada* in the house but they are welcome to make *posada* in the stable. The doors are flung open, all are invited to enter, and song and dance erupt. Children take swings at piñatas and scramble for the fruit, sugar cane, peanuts, and candy that come cascading down. *Las Posadas*.

What a wonderful way to teach children that hospitality lies at the heart of Christmas. They experience firsthand the refusal of shelter for eight days before tasting the sweetness of welcome. They experience a world that fears the stranger and believes them to be scoundrels. They experience closed doors, unwelcome, inhospitality. Children are given a crash course in the kind of world that Jesus entered and that we live in today.

God has found hospitality in Mary's womb and now walks the streets of Bethlehem, seeking it elsewhere. Will God sleep in the streets on his birth night? The innkeeper redeems humanity with a welcome to a stable—most likely a cave. And God's first breath of human air is a mixture of field hay, animal poop, damp earth, and cold cave. Welcome home, God.

It doesn't get much better. Before Jesus is out of diapers, he's a refugee on the run from Herod. He flees to Egypt (most likely as an undocumented person) and makes his home far from family and friends. He lives in a land that does not hold good memories for his people. Later in his life, Jesus will say that he has no place to lay his head. He travels from city to city, dependent on the hospitality of others. At his death, he is laid to rest in a borrowed tomb, thanks to the hospitality of Joseph of Arimathea. From a first cave to a last cave are the lodgings of the Savior. In the words of John's Gospel, "He came to that which was his own, but his own did not receive him" (1:11). Here is God—homeless, a vagrant, a refugee, needing bed and bath and meal—finally buried in a borrowed tomb. We humans can be downright inhospitable.

GOING DEEPER

This same God provided *posada* to us—a garden with food, water, air, shelter, safety, clothes, companionship. God thought of everything we needed and shared it freely. What a gracious host. And even there in the garden, we raided God's tree to rid ourselves of dependency on God's hospitality. And again, in the exodus from Egypt, God provided manna and quail, water flowing from rocks, guiding beacons in the sky, *posada* in the wilderness. Then God led us to a land flowing with milk and honey, figs and pomegranates.

The story of Jesus is part of the ongoing story of the hospitality of God: baptizing us into a family with a warm bath, feeding us at his table, standing on the front porch waiting for the wayward to come home, and going to prepare a place for us that has many rooms.

In the first century, one of the distinctive practices of Christianity was hospitality. They offered food and shelter, help for the needy, safe places, open arms, open tables, open doors. As people watched this practice of the early Christians, they saw likeness to God.

Sometime, somewhere, the parade of wandering humanity will come to your door asking for *posada*. They will need your resources, your space, your time, your help, your home. In offering *posada* to the least of these, you are offering it to Jesus.

The old hymn "Thou Didst Leave Thy Throne" is a wonderful reminder of God seeking entrance. Tell each other stories of local, undocumented persons in your community, or invite leaders of immigrant communities to join your study. Allow the story of Jesus to grow beyond the cozy comfort of a closed stable.

CONSIDER THIS

1. This is the only text in all of Scripture that tells of Jesus being born in a stable. How does the Gospel of Luke seem to be the fitting place for this story?

2. What other stories in Luke focus on strangers, outsiders, and excluded persons?

3. The companion book for Luke is Acts. How does the emphasis on strangers, outsiders, and excluded persons continue there?

4. Describe a time when you were a stranger. How were you given *posada* (or not)?

5. How does today's devotional reflection and scriptural text alter the way you think about Christmas?

4

THREE CHEERS FOR
RELIGIOUS RITUAL

SCRIPTURE

Luke 2:21–52

THE BIG IDEA

Religious ritual gets a bad rap these days. But we find it in full force in this text. Grounding children in the ways of God's people makes good sense. As we pattern ourselves after the story of God, this is an essential message for parents.

CORE TEACHING

As Christmas goes, we quickly get Jesus in a manger and Mary pondering these things in her heart. And the next thing we know, Christmas is put way until next year and Jesus is thirty years old and being baptized in the Jordan. From baby to grown man in just a few short verses.

Today's scripture invites us to slow down a bit and look into the practices that began to form Jesus. Luke invites us into the Jewish world of religious ceremony and observance of the Law. He writes about circumcision, purification, dedication, naming, consecration, and ceremonial festivals. All of these rituals are packed into one text. Jesus grew up in the context of religious practices.

Spiritual formation is essential during the first eighteen years if our children are to embrace the faith we hold dear. Apparently, God intends that families of faith observe formative practices. In these years, a value system is adopted, a worldview internalized, expectations established, respect learned, and self-image formed. And who our children grow up around is just as important. Role models can speak instruction, grace, and blessing into the heart of a child.

Luke tells us that Jesus was growing up wise, strong, and favored by God and humans. We conclude that the way Mary and Joseph attended religious obligation had something to do with this. They believed their child belonged to God, and so Jesus was circumcised and thus given the mark of the covenant people. The center of gravity for the family was the gathering place of the people of God. No place was more important than the temple (or synagogue). No people were more important than the worshiping community. No day was more important than the Sabbath. No words were more important than Scripture. Here we find Mary and Joseph repeatedly at the synagogue, performing the rituals, keeping the Law, offering sacrifice.

And along the way, they receive two gifts. An old man named Simeon takes the child in his arms and speaks prophetically of the saving work of God to be done through this child. He speaks of Jesus as a light to the gentiles, not a common thing to be heard in a Jewish synagogue. And then an old woman named Anna comes along and also makes a fuss about the child while praising God for the gift of this baby. The older generation sees in the child the activity of God in the world.

Don't miss what Luke is preparing us to understand—that, out of the historic Jewish faith with its laws, rituals, and ways, comes a Savior of the gentiles. You can't get any more Jewish than this text, yet it points us beyond the people who already know God to the people who don't. Luke is not disrespectful to Jewish ways and customs. He connects Jesus to them in every way. Yet he offers the story and life of Jesus to the whole world.

The closing story of Jesus with the elders in the temple demonstrates the same tension. Jesus is in the temple hearing the old stories while preparing himself to live out his Father's new mission.

Parents need to hear this text for the sake of their children. In a busy world, we often fail to grasp the power of repeated ritual for the spiritual formation of our children.

GOING DEEPER

While Luke's function in this text is to connect the Jewish roots of Jesus to the Gentile mission, the text also recognizes the formative influence of religious ritual as part of the identity of a child being formed for service to God.

Fred Craddock tells the story of an encounter between a parent and a pastor. The conversation goes like this:

Parent: "Let's see, was it next Sunday that my daughter was going to be baptized?"

Pastor: "Yes, next Sunday."

"Well . . . she has dance lessons next Sunday."

"Well, the baptism is Sunday morning."

"Well, the dance lessons are at 10:30."

"On Sunday morning?"

"Yeah. The dance studio has lessons on Sunday morning."

"Then we have a decision to make, don't we?"[1]

That's what we have as parents: decisions to make about religious rituals that are formative. We root our children in the old ways to prepare them to be God's gift to the whole world. We teach them who and whose they are before sending them into adulthood. This is the story of Jesus. It can be our story too.

Discuss what infant baptism or dedication means to you. Does the Sunday school program in your church offer a catechism for children?

A wonderful accompanying story can be found in Anne Lamott's book *Traveling Mercies* in the chapter titled "Why I Make Sam Go to Church."

CONSIDER THIS

1. What are the primary practices of the church today that rise from the Jewish rites of circumcision and purification?

2. This is the only text in all of Scripture that speaks of Jesus as a growing child. Why do other Gospels not do this? Why is this particular story essential to Luke's larger story?

3. How does the temple visit in Luke 2:41–52 round out today's scriptural passage?

4. If you could offer any wisdom to young parents today regarding the spiritual formation of their children, what would you say?

5. What kind of teenager do you think Jesus was?

---

1. Fred B. Craddock, *Craddock Stories*. Edited by Mike Graves and Richard F. Ward (St. Louis: Chalice Press, 2001), 51.

WILDERNESS CONFESSIONAL BOOTH

SCRIPTURE

Luke 3:1–20

THE BIG IDEA

The coming of Jesus makes all things new. Life is viewed from a different perspective that can only be grasped through the practice of repentance.

CORE TEACHING

John the Baptist is out in the wilderness. The people of God have been here before. He is preaching a baptism that involves repentance. He's not your average evangelist. No Armani suits, Rolex watches, 1-800 contribution numbers, CDs of recorded sermons to sell, or amphitheaters to preach from. He's wearing dead animal pelts and eating desert *du jour*. And crowds are coming out to be baptized by him. But

John doesn't necessarily seem to be glad about the crowds. His words seem to indicate a foul mood. He calls them names: vipers, name-droppers, deadwood, coat hoarders, tax collectors, extortionists. These are not exactly part of a list of best preaching practices if you want a congregation next week.

In fact, John reminds me of another evangelist. Remember Jonah, the Old Testament preacher who was sent to Nineveh with the offer of forgiveness? His message went something like this: "God is coming to judge your sin and wickedness. Repent—or else! There's nobody here who wants salvation, is there? I didn't think so. I'm outta here. See ya."

Just about the time John is ready to pack up his wilderness confessional booth, a line starts forming for baptism. John tells them that their Jewish ancestry is worthless if they want to keep sinning against their fellow humans. The ax of judgment is aimed at the root of that tree. Apparently, salvation has come in a new way through a Messiah yet to be identified. John is the forerunner of this announcement. The wilderness congregation asks what they should do. John gives them three snapshots of what repentance might look like.

First, the people with more than enough coats should share with those who don't have enough coats. This sounds a lot like the earlier wilderness story, when manna fell from heaven and everyone went out to collect. The one who gathered much did not have too much, and the one who gathered little did not have too little. There is equity of provision in the coming kingdom. It all begins with the way the people of God view their possessions. When our brother has too little and we have too much, helping is where repentance begins.

Second, some of the people appealed to Herod's government for the privilege of collecting taxes from their brothers and sisters. The highest bidders got the job. They were free to gouge their fellow humans for all they could collect, with Herod's military backing. Once they had satisfied Herod by meeting the bid, they could keep whatever was left over. The tax collectors wanted to know what repentance looked like for them. John answered: Collect no more than what is required. Be fair. Show consideration. Clean up your act. Live with dignity among your neighbors. Be known for your just ways.

Third, some of the people were Jewish mercenary soldiers who had been hired by Herod and assigned to local patrols. Because they were given such power, they could invade homes, threaten people, take what they wanted, and command what they wished. Repentance for them meant no extortion, no theft, and no strong-arm tactics. Be satisfied with their pay. Treat their neighbors with dignity and not force.

Can you imagine such a world? No one hungry or cold. Fair and just use of power. No military coercion. Peace on earth, good will toward all. This is the world of which we dream. And Jesus comes to offer it. John tells us we need to repent of our old ways in order to receive the gift of a new world. We cannot keep on doing the same old things and expect the kingdom to fit into the world we've created. The kingdom requires us to change.

GOING DEEPER

A companion story to this devotional reflection is found in Donald Miller's book *Blue Like Jazz*. He tells the story of students at Reed College building a confessional booth on campus during the height of a hedonist festival called Renn

Fayre. The twist in the story is that the booth is set up for *Christians* to confess. They ask forgiveness from the party crowd for their failure to live like Jesus on the campus. It is a great reminder that repentance begins in the house of God.[1]

Salvation heals the wrongs that we inflict on each other. The coming of Jesus addresses a complex world of taxes, power, and possessions.

CONSIDER THIS.

1. What are some current examples of coats, taxes, and military power?

2. How is John like Isaiah? Why does Luke liken John to the work of Isaiah?

3. How does this kingdom ethic begin to have overtones of Jesus's gentile mission?

4. Is repentance still practiced today in our church gatherings? How?

5. If John the Baptist were preaching in town this weekend, what would he say?

---

1. Donald Miller, *Blue Like Jazz: Non-Religious Thoughts on Christian Spirituality* (Nashville: Thomas Nelson, 2003).

KNOWING WHO YOU ARE

SCRIPTURE

Luke 3:21–4:15

THE BIG IDEA

The identity and mission of Jesus are the focus of these scriptural passages. At his baptism, the Father identifies Jesus as the beloved Son. In Luke's genealogy, Jesus's lineage is traced all the way back to Adam via Abraham, affirming the identity of Jesus as the one through whom all the nations of the earth will be blessed. A study of the genealogy will reveal intentional effort on Luke's part to broaden the Jewish tree to include the promise to the whole world. In the story of the temptations in the wilderness, the devil attempts to draw Jesus into other identities by offering different paths to fulfill his mission. It is clear that Jesus knows who he is and that he resists each temptation on the basis of the mission of God.

CORE TEACHING

Identity can be formed in two ways. We can aspire to be someone or something and live toward that goal, knowing that when we achieve it, people will identify us by our accomplishments. This is a common way of living and being. People every day are trying to make something of themselves, trying to be somebody. They are living *toward* an identity. This can be motivating, but it can also be disastrous because, until you become somebody, your identity remains in question. And if you fail, who are you?

Luke presents Jesus in a different way. Jesus is *given* an identity. We have seen it in the angel's visit to Mary, in the song of the holy mother, at his birth announcement to shepherds, in the temple with the elders, at his baptism by the Father, and in Luke's genealogy. We are told who Jesus is before he does anything significant. Identity can be earned, but it can also be given. Jesus's identity is given to him.

GOING DEEPER

I was given an identity. Rather than telling me what I could become, my parents told me who I was. They repeatedly told me the stories of our family, how we lived and acted. They took me to church a week after I was born and began inducting me into the people of God. Before I headed out for weekend fun, my dad always reminded me, "Don't forget. You're a Boone." I knew how Boones lived and how they didn't. Temptation was not a hard thing to handle because I knew who I was.

After three chapters of telling us who Jesus is, we see the test in Luke 4. The devil encounters Jesus in the wilderness and tests him at three missional points. The temptations are essentially alternate ways to carry out the mission of God. Feed yourself from these stones, gain glory for

yourself, and do something spectacular to prove yourself.
Jesus resists each one in favor of feeding on the words of the
Father, bringing glory to the Father, and not tempting the
Father to catch him.

It is better to know who we are in Christ and to live out
of this secure identity than it is to try to make something
of ourselves. Being who you are in Christ is better than
becoming someone else. Identity is a gift.

Each of Jesus's three temptations has an Old Testament
basis. Review the background for each in the accompanying texts. You can project each temptation into the stories
of Luke that will follow. Jesus feeds multitudes with little
less than stones (Luke 9). Jesus deflects glory to the Father.
And Jesus asks to be saved from the fate of death but is not
caught by angels (Luke 22).

Another theme found here is the role of the Holy Spirit
in the life and ministry of Jesus. The Gospel of Luke leaves
the reader with no question about how Jesus did what he
did. With almost every action, Luke writes, "and Jesus,
filled with the Holy Spirit . . ." It all began with the Spirit-
filled conception announcement to Mary: "The Holy Spirit
will come on you, and the power of the Most High will
overshadow you" (Luke 1:35). And the Gospel ends with
the promised gift from the Father, the Holy Spirit, who was
waiting for the disciples in Jerusalem.

It is not surprising then that the temptations of Jesus
occur under the filling of the Spirit. Jesus is led by the Spirit
to an abandoned, lifeless, death zone called the desert. Such
a place was the home of Israel for forty years of wilderness
wandering. No wonder it becomes the home of the devil
himself when he tries to distract Jesus from the work of the
Father with a tantalizing offer. The same devil draws us
to desert places and promises us empty pursuits. And the

same Holy Spirit frequents our deserts and empowers us to say a firm no. This Spirit is everywhere.

CONSIDER THIS

1. Investigate the genealogy of Jesus. Who are these people, and what does this family tree suggest?

2. Explore the Old Testament references in the temptations. Read the entire psalm that each quote is taken from. How does knowing the context of the entire psalm inform the understanding of the basis of the temptation?

3. Can you find the humor in Jesus's response to the third temptation? It takes the Old Testament context to figure it out.

4. Do you have a secure identity, or are you trying hard to be somebody?

TOUCHED

SCRIPTURE

Luke 4:16–30

THE BIG IDEA

The ministry of Jesus, when fully understood, cuts into our comfort zone and asks us to go places we would never willingly choose to go.

CORE TEACHING

(This is offered in a first-person narrative. Imagine you are hearing it from the perspective of a citizen of Nazareth.)[1]

---

1. Excerpted from Dan Boone, *Preaching the Story that Shapes Us* (Kansas City, MO: Beacon Hill Press of Kansas City, 2008), 213–18. Edited and used by permission.

We Nazarenes tried to kill Jesus. No foolin'. Our city was built on a cliff. Nazareth. And Jesus made us mad enough to kill him, or at least try. It happened like this. We knew he was special early on. *Touched*. Not the kind of touched that lands you in the psych ward but the kind of touched that says heaven has something invested in this one. He was a Spirit baby—part Mary, part God, but *all* Jesus of Nazareth, or Jesus the Nazarene. Important people said important words over him before he could walk.

Profound words make you watch a kid closer. His being from Nazareth wasn't exactly a plus. Nazareth is a hick town, a one-horse, two-bit village. When the word *Nazarene* came up in conversation, people over in Capernaum would say, "Can anything good come out of Nazareth?" Our civic pride was . . . well, it was no great honor to be from Nazareth. We did our best. And Jesus grew up in our hometown.

I remember the year we all went to Jerusalem for Passover. Most of us who made the trek were kin, so we watched after each other's kids. Well, Jesus got absorbed talking with the teachers at the temple. Even *they* knew this kid was touched. Twelve-year-old boys are usually more interested in sticks and snakes than in holy law. He called it his Father's business. He knew what he was about at twelve.

About age thirty, his cousin John baptized him. That's when we knew he was definitely touched—the Holy Spirit just dropped down on him like a diving dove, and he started going places—teaching, healing, and doing things only God can do. He had this energy working inside him. He was popular. Everybody said great things about him. We kept reading the reports in the *Nazarene Gazette*. "Nazarene Packs Galilee Civic Center." "Nazarene Heals Town Sick." "Nazarene Feeds Mini-City with Mini-Meal." Our own town rag sported the headline, "Local Boy Makes Good!"

Then he came home. Local pride swelled. We had a bona fide hero. A God-touched, divinely energized, heaven-powered, Holy Spirited, anointed prophet . . . from Nazareth. Welcome home, Jesus! The relatives were thrilled. Their stock had gone up in town. And now when somebody mentioned Nazareth, they'd say, "Isn't that where Jesus is from?" Nazareth might well ride Jesus's popular coattails to a new level of honor and respectability. Welcome home, Jesus!

We honored him at the synagogue on the Sabbath by asking him to read from the scroll of the prophet Isaiah. He wasted no time browsing, rolled it right to the section he knew he wanted to read. They were words of great promise to Jews. "The Spirit of the Lord is upon me because he has anointed me to bring good news to the poor. He has commissioned me to proclaim release to captives, recovery of sight to blind, freedom for the oppressed, to proclaim that now is the year of the Lord's favor." He rolled the scroll up, handed it to the attendant, and sat down.

No comment? Every eye in the place was on him. Certainly he'd done more than this in Capernaum and throughout Galilee. Silence hung across the room. Then he said, "Today . . . this scripture has been fulfilled in your hearing." What gracious words. What audience command. Jesus was certainly headed toward a key to the city and a street named after him.

The buzz of approval did a wave around the synagogue. You could hear them. "Joseph's boy. I remember when he was knee high to a grasshopper." "I was the one who found him when he got left at the temple in Jerusalem." "Well, I was there when that dove landed on him in the river."

I was thinking, *Now Jesus, we're ready for good news to low-esteem Nazarenes. Maybe a word about release from Roman oppression? That'll get some fervent political blood behind you.*

Or a healing for a blind person right here in Nazareth! Do your stuff. Let us see the favor of God hitting Nazareth in tangible form. Visions of grandeur danced in our heads! We had years of hoping hanging on a local hero.

That's when he turned on us. We were stunned. At first we didn't get it. He said, "In a few minutes you'll probably be quoting me one of your Proverbs, like, 'Doctor, cure yourself.' You'll think I'm *touched*, all right. The kind of touched that lands you in a psych ward. You'll say, 'You better work a miracle on yourself.'"

Was he joking? It wasn't funny. He continued.

"You're here today to see some Holy Spirit razzle-dazzle. You want a spiritual buzz. I'm good for your image. I make you look better. Truth is, you're not really interested in my Father's business. You despise the people he's after: sinners, pagans, outsiders, gentiles. Your hearts are too narrow to get your arms around them. You're here because you think I can do things for you that you can't do for yourself. You see me as a hometown boy who owes you a divine favor, a miracle, a dose of status."

We couldn't believe what we were hearing. The homecoming was quickly unraveling. This was getting ugly. We didn't like being talked to this way by Joseph's son. Now, maybe he had a point. Maybe we were there to up our status. Maybe we did think he owed us a few favors, seeing how he was on the *in* with God. Maybe we did have expectations of fast miracles and political freedom and heavenly blessings. But doesn't everybody who goes to the synagogue? Don't we all want to be close enough to spiritual power to ask an occasional favor? What's so wrong with hoping God will endorse your agenda?

You people here today aren't so different from my Nazareth clan. You don't show up all sold out to loving people you despise. You don't beg to have your heart stretched to embrace people you'd rather avoid. You're here because you don't have power to make life happen like you want it to. You need help. But take it from me. This Jesus isn't a puppet on a string. He's no divinely powered bellhop.

Let me get on with what happened next. He said, "A prophet has no honor in his hometown." That was a no-brainer. Then he drove the nail in his own coffin. He talked about two prophets: Elijah, during the three-and-a-half-year drought, and how God did not send him to the widows in Israel but to a pagan widow of Zarephath; and Elisha, who—with Jewish lepers on every corner—went to Syria looking for a military enemy named Namaan. Of all the nerve!

Last straw! He announces all these good things God has energized and anointed him to do, but he refuses to do them in his own hometown! He is going to sinners, outsiders, and gentiles. Everybody is talking all at once. If we Nazarenes stretch that far, we'll break. Our town already is shamed. What will people think of us if our finest citizen spends his life giving God's gifts to pagans? They're not worthy of miracles. We are! We've got to get this Jesus under control. He's wasting the anointing on gentiles. This cannot be! The son of Joseph is out of control. He will leave our town and spread this nonsense to other villages. We'll be the laughingstock of religion—again!

There was a rage in the synagogue that day. We rushed him, drove him to the edge of town, toward the bluff. One well-deserved push would be the end of him. But it never happened. He left town and took his anointing with him. He never came back. A time or two some of his relatives went out after him. I think they thought he was *touched*.

We tried to get on with life, but we kept hearing reports. He had collected some rather ordinary followers. He traveled from city to city with his unimpressive entourage. He had no backing from religious authorities. All he had was the touch, the anointing, of God. His touch drove demons out of people. His touch stopped bleeding inside a woman. His touch brought blush back into the cheeks of a little girl headed for the cemetery. His touch made a sightless man see. His touch gave political crooks a reason to go straight.

I guess if he had stayed in our Nazareth synagogue, none of this would have happened. He made a lot of people glad—people who would never have thought of darkening the door of our synagogue. But he made a lot of people mad too. Pharisees, scribes, wealthy rulers, Sadducees. They knew all the rules, doctrine, and tradition. But he had the anointing, the touch of God. And with needy people, the anointing wins hands down.

So they did him in. They finished what we couldn't do that day in Nazareth. They snuffed his spirit, annulled his anointing, retired his touch. They killed him.

Strange thing, though. I heard the other day that 120 of his followers were praying together, not asking for personal favors but asking for the gift of the Spirit. And they were touched, anointed, divinely energized, Spirit-filled. I'm talking men *and* women, young *and* old, Jews *and* gentiles. And they've been touching people in Jerusalem, Judea, Samaria—all over the world.

But back to my hometown. That day we tried to throw him off the cliff, he walked right through us and out of town. Something in me was saying, "Follow him, follow him." But I let my desire for status stop me. And my prejudice against sinners. And my selfish interests.

I've always wondered what it would take for a guy like me to follow a man like him. How could I ever love sinners the way he does? I suppose I'd have to be touched.

GOING DEEPER

What is the agenda of your local congregation? Are you engaged in the announced mission of Jesus or just asking God to endorse your religious wishes? I often think the church saddens God when the bride of his Son gives herself to all kinds of things that have nothing to do with the mission of the kingdom. The same Jesus who walked away from his hometown may do the same on his church today unless we open ourselves to the announced mission of God.

Dare we say, "The Spirit of the Lord is on [us] because he has anointed [us] to proclaim good news to the poor. He has sent [us] to proclaim freedom for the prisoners and recovery of sight for the blind, to set the oppressed free, to proclaim the year of the Lord's favor" (Luke 4:18–19).

Luke is once again noting the radical nature of the messianic mission to the gentiles by giving us a glimpse of Jesus in his hometown. How does the mission of God call your church beyond its comfort zone?

CONSIDER THIS

1. Have you ever been jealous of the grace that supposedly undeserving people experience even while faithful churchgoers seem to pray in for their own miracles?

2. How does Luke prepare us for the rest of the Gospel in this story?

3. Compare this story to Acts 2. What similarities do you find?

4. What does it mean to be Spirit-anointed?

SABBATH DEBATES

SCRIPTURE

Luke 5:33–6:11

THE BIG IDEA

Two boundary markers for Judaism are fasting and Sabbath observance. Tucked in the middle of chapters devoted to calling the Twelve are these three anecdotes about how the practices of Jesus and his disciples, contrary to typical Jewish customs, aggravate the Pharisees, who have historically viewed themselves as guardians of Jewish religious tradition.

CORE TEACHING

There is a debate about the practices of the disciples of Jesus. They seem to be doing a lot more eating and drinking than fasting and praying. Jesus notes that neither eating and drinking, nor fasting and praying, is wrong. It's just that Jesus is inaugurating a new kingdom, which calls for practices that are in keeping with the kingdom that is coming.

The illustration of wine and wineskins is essentially a parable of appropriateness. The practices that are appropriate to the new kingdom are eating and drinking. The bridegroom of the coming kingdom is among the disciples now, therefore it is appropriate to eat, drink, and celebrate. Soon enough he will be gone, and they will await his return. At that point it will be appropriate for them to fast and pray.

This minor complaint becomes a larger issue when the Pharisees note that Jesus's disciples also break Sabbath law by "harvesting" heads of grain on the Sabbath. In response to this, Jesus cites Old Testament precedent, recalling a time when David and his friends were given the bread of presence—which, by law, was only supposed to be eaten by the priests. Yet God provided for David and his men in their time of need. As Jesus shares this story, we hear faint echoes from that Old Testament story that indicate something similar is happening in this text. Jesus is the messianic King David, and these are his men, his disciples. Their needs are being met by the grain available in the unharvested field.

The strongest statement is made by Jesus in Luke 6:5: "The Son of Man is Lord of the Sabbath." In other Gospels we hear that the Sabbath is made for man, not man for the Sabbath. In other words, the Sabbath is meant to be a gift more so than an obligation.

The story continues as Jesus heals a man with a withered hand on the Sabbath, to the displeasure of the scribes and Pharisees. We feel the tension in the room as Luke describes the way Jesus is watched to see whether he'll heal the man's hand. And Jesus knows what they are thinking, so he addresses them with a rhetorical question and then heals the man anyway. Those watching, predictably, become enraged.

What is it about religion that finds more delight in making boxes to put people in rather than finding ways to get people out of boxes? The scribes and Pharisees saw the Law first and humans second. They insisted that their disciples observe the laws of fasting and prayer, avoid undue celebration, go hungry if need be while walking through a grain field on the Sabbath, and put an illness on hold for twenty-four hours. They saw the Law as preeminent, always.

Jesus, on the other hand, saw the *people* to whom the Law was given as the object of God's primary concern. Thus, his disciples celebrated the arrival of a new kingdom. If they were on a journey with Jesus and grew hungry, they were allowed to rub heads of grain between their hands and enjoy God's bounty. If they encountered a man with a deformed hand and had it in their capacity to help him, they would, regardless of which day of the week it happened to be. Jesus saw needy people trapped in boxes and liberated them. The Pharisees built boxes and attempted to confine people in them.

GOING DEEPER

This conversation seems to come down to the issue of authority. In most religious groups, there is concern about getting people to behave as directed. And this concern is not all bad. The people of God have always observed practices that help us experience God. But Jesus uses his God-given authority to meet the needs of people. When he declares himself Lord of the Sabbath, he is speaking with an authority that feeds the hungry, heals the sick, and welcomes the new kingdom. This is a very different authority than the one that forces people to jump through hoops of your own making as nothing more than confirmation of your authority over them. The authority that interests Jesus is the authority to liberate people.

We walk a fine line between being dismissive of the practices of the Christian life (prayer, fasting, Sabbath observance) and supporting the practices while keeping them in the right perspective. The practices are given to us to structure our lives for service to God and others, not to prohibit us from serving others.

CONSIDER THIS

1. How will eating and drinking become symbols of the coming kingdom in the Gospel of Luke?

2. Is Sabbath law still important? Why or why not?

3. Where have you seen Pharisees in our world today?

4. In these texts, Luke gives us several hints that Jesus is more than just a traveling prophet. What are these hints?

HOLLOW LAUGHTER, HOLY TEARS

SCRIPTURE

Luke 6:17–26

THE BIG IDEA

The coming of Jesus is a reversal of fortunes in both directions. In scripture, a blessing is a set of words invested with the power to do good. The blessing's dark cousin, the curse, is a set of words invested with the power to harm. In the Old Testament, words are deeds. They go out from the one who speaks them and cause something to happen, for good or bad. The word of the Lord created the world. The curse of Balaam put a whammy on the military might of tribes. Words *do* things. Blessing and curse are defined in this scripture as laughing and weeping.

By the time of Jesus, the world was made up of those who were blessed by God (with money, status, power, religious acceptance into the temple pecking order, a pure lineage, maleness) and those who felt cursed by God (tax collectors, prostitutes, the lepers, the sick, the disabled, sheep herders, women) because they were barred from blessing. And along came Jesus announcing a new sheriff in town. He introduced a new reign. Characteristic of this new kingdom was a reversal of fortunes. Outsiders were in for good news. This was their lucky day because the kingdom of God had come for the likes of them.

CORE TEACHING[1]

Listen. Do you hear someone crying?

A people down in Egypt being manhandled by Pharaoh.

A man named Jeremiah, heartbroken over the moral slide of his people, cries from his prison slime-pit, "Oh, that my head were a spring of water, and my eyes a fountain of tears!" (Jeremiah 9:1).

Jesus sits on a hill overlooking Jerusalem. Peace is knocking at the door. No one answers. Can you hear his tears?

In Auschwitz, in Selma, and in Darfur, the crushing weight of an old world's sinful use of power. Can you hear them weep?

Divorce papers are coldly served. She sobs.

A believer has finally gotten honest about his addictive sin. He tries to shake it and falls back into the trap, again. He cries.

A woman foregoes her career to stay home. She pours her life into her children. No one sees the table games she

1. Dan Boone, *Preaching the Story that Shapes Us* (Kansas City, MO: Beacon Hill Press of Kansas City, 2008), 224–29. Edited and used by permission.

played with them, the life lessons she taught, the bedtime Bible stories she read. And her neighbors, the working women, make her feel devalued, unproductive, used by her husband. She has no office, no plaques, no salary, no recognizable societal value. She weeps.

A parent sits in a dark family room on a Saturday night. An independent teenager is out there somewhere, doing something. The father remembers other, younger days, when they laughed and played and talked. Now the relationship is one long argument. He weeps in the silence of the family room, waiting for the sound of the car.

A young, thirty-something businessman did not get the promotion. He knows why. He isn't a drinkin' buddy with the boss, has no "killer instinct," wasn't willing to sacrifice his family on the company altar. It is obvious that his relationship with God has cost him cold, hard cash. He's not the emotional type, but today he cries.

An employee is summoned to an office by other employees to clean up a mess they made. She knows it's a pecking-order game. They can tell her what to do. The family image in this company lasts about as long as it takes to say, "cheese." She cleans up the mess with a servant spirit. They stand snickering. A tear edges to the corner of her eye.

Teenagers like to be out on Friday night. The guy she likes is out with someone who does not have such strict convictions. She's at home, crying.

Weeping. Do you hear it? The weeping of people on the bottom. Tears of the humble, broken, and powerless. This upside-down world has fallen hard on them, and it squeezes tears from their souls. Reality stinks! And they weep.

But it is hard to hear the bottom half cry over the noisy laughter coming from the top half. Laughter always drowns out weeping, except maybe in the ears of God.

Can you hear the laughter?

It's coming from Pharaoh's palace as he tells the good ol' boys that he is going to raise the brick quota on the Hebrew slaves.

It's the laughter of the men who tossed old Jeremiah in slime pit. They are sick of his moralizing.

It's the laughter of Pharisees, Sadducees, and the Council on Friday night as they mimic the words and deeds of a crucified man who will not give them any more trouble.

A preacher laughs. He has built a big church around his ego, has mastered the art of image control and people pleasing. He picks on the little people with an air of disdain. At conventions he is a religious rock star.

The office manager and "the boys" are discussing how to get rid of their fifty-something secretary and replace her with someone more pleasing to their eyes.

People laugh in bedrooms after ten p.m. as the late-show hosts dismantle public people in their monologues.

Guys on a golf course chuckle as another ethnic joke is told loudly enough to be overheard.

The free-as-a-bird man is bragging about the alimony settlement. His lawyer got him everything and left her with next to nothing. He laughs with his smug attorney over a beer in a bar.

Can you hear the laughter? It is the laughter from the top of an upside-down world. The laughter of people who have settled down comfortably. Lost the capacity to be touched. Learned to shrug and say, "Business is business." It is the laughter of people who no longer grieve injustice or wince when somebody does somebody else wrong. It is the laughter of people who have lost the capacity to weep.

Some of it is the laughter of churchgoing people who've carved out a comfortable niche behind pat answers, moral judgments, and religious clichés. People who have not been touched in years by the tears of a poor person, a suicidal teenager, an agonizing homosexual, or a lonely shut-in. It is too much to be weighed down by such people.

So, the world laughs on. Can you hear it?

But something is missing in this laughter. It is a throat laugh, not a soulful, belly laugh. A hollow, empty, forced laugh. A callous, cold, hard laugh.

Jesus stood before his followers and made plain statements of fact: Blessed are those who weep. They will laugh. Cursed are those who laugh now. They will weep.

He must be talking about a new world because this old, upside-down world doesn't pin a *blessed* label on divorced people, broken addicts, stay-at-home moms, parents agonizing over lost kids, blackballed Christian businessmen, and low-pecking-order people. They are cursed. The world suggests they get a good lawyer and sue somebody up on top. But Jesus says they are blessed because they weep. They are humble. They are holy.

If you ask me, Jesus puts the planet on a greased swivel pin and turns it right side up. The laugh-happy upper crust topples. The weeping bottom rises.

Not everybody sees or hears it, but it is happening. A new, right-side-up world is being born. A holy world of hearty laughter. And this new world has laughter and weeping too.

Listen. Can you hear the weeping?

It's the weeping from Egypt, where every firstborn has died and Pharaoh has drowned in the Red Sea.

It's the weeping of Jeremiah's peers whose lives have crumbled in moral decay.

It's the weeping of Pharisees, Sadducees, and the Council as they realize that dead Messiahs don't always stay dead and their power is demolished by resurrection.

It's the weeping of slave owners and power barons who did as they pleased with people.

It's the weeping of pecking-order players, sharp-tongued piranha, and top-of-the-world manipulators.

It's the weeping of churchgoing folk with sufficient Bible knowledge but insufficient compassion.

It's the weeping of pleasure seekers and voyagers after money, sex, and power.

It's the weeping of people who refused to hear the truth about themselves or listen to the cries they caused.

Can you hear it? The hollow laughter has turned on its head, and the painful reality of having lived upside down is expressed in weeping. Can you hear it? It's hard to hear it because, in this new world, the laughter is much louder than in the old.

It's the laughter of slaves leaving Egypt.

It's the laughter of disciples beholding a risen Lord.

It's the laughter of a woman who moves past an ugly divorce whole, forgiving, and at peace among the people of God.

It's the laughter of a sinner who confessed and repented, and is now developing new and holy habits.

It's the laughter of a mother who stayed at home and poured her life into her children and watched that investment yield eternal dividends. She could not be prouder of who they have become.

It's the laughter of a dad whose wayward teen came home and straightened up.

It's the laughter of a woman who embraces her non-promoted husband and says, "I'd rather have *you* than all the money you'd earn by being somewhere else all week with the company. I'm proud of you!"

It's the laughter of a low-pecking-order employee whose self-worth doesn't come from whom she can boss around but from the God who has placed value upon her.

It's the laughter of a teen turned young bride on her wedding night. The passion is pure. There are no regrets. She is glad she saved herself for him and he for her.

Can you hear this laughter? It is the laughter of a new, right-side-up world. It is the laughter of those who have the last laugh—an eternal laugh.

Blessed are those who have capacity to weep now. They will laugh! Cursed are those who coldly laugh now. They will weep!

GOING DEEPER

In the new deal called the kingdom of God, blessing is offered to those who never considered themselves eligible. This new arrangement is not about a socialist state, where the playing field is leveled by the government and everyone gets the same paycheck. Nor is it about the evils of being wealthy, fed, and happy. It is about access to the blessing of God. The religious system of Jesus's day denied access to certain classes and groups of people. They lived under the belief that God hated them. Jesus brought good news to everyone. Well, maybe not everyone. Those who built religious fences to protect their own interests at the expense of their neighbor would find themselves misaligned with the new kingdom.

Read Matthew 23, and note how Jesus confronts self-serving religion.

CONSIDER THIS

1. Who is crying in your world? Why?

2. Who is laughing? About what?

3. When will the world be made right?

4. How can Christians begin to participate in the coming kingdom now?

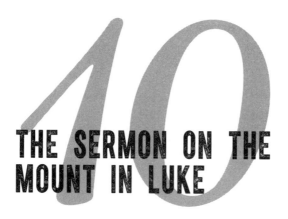

THE SERMON ON THE MOUNT IN LUKE

SCRIPTURE

Luke 6:27–49

THE BIG IDEA

In 6:17–19, Luke introduces a section of teaching that is found in Matthew 5–7 and is commonly known as the Sermon on the Mount. While some of the same elements are found in both, the setting is a little different, and the note of Jesus's authority comes at the beginning in Luke (6:19) but at the end in Matthew (7:28–29). Not all of Matthew's account is found here, but what is present seems to focus on the radical nature of the kingdom—loving one's enemies, avoiding hypocrisy by not judging, valuing a person by the fruit they bear, and securing one's life on a solid foundation.

CORE TEACHING

Luke 6:27–36. In Matthew, this is the fifth of Jesus's "You have heard it said, but" teachings. Luke, however, uses only this one, and doesn't even include that language. It is reminiscent of the acts of repentance named by John the Baptist in Luke 3:10–14. The standard for loving enemies is the Father. As the Most High is kind to the ungrateful and the wicked, so are we to be. In this way, we reveal our lineage. Luke abounds with illustrations of Jesus loving the enemy, but nowhere is the example as succinct as Jesus praying from the cross, "Father, forgive them."

An interesting note is the comparison of the closing of Matthew's account and Luke's account. Matthew ends by calling us to be perfect as our Father in heaven is perfect. This is about being holy as God is holy—not absolute perfection but fulfilling our Creator's desires for us, functioning as we are called to function. Luke, on the other hand, ends with "be merciful, just as your Father is merciful" (6:36). Could it be that, for Luke, the essence of holiness is mercy—the offering of the other cheek, the coat, a blessing in exchange for cursing, and kindness to enemies? In a tit-for-tat world of religious measurements and purity codes, such behavior would stand out like a Mercedes in a Subaru lot.

Luke 6:37–42. A similar thought continues in this section. Blind to our own sin, how can we guide others toward where they should go? Pharisees were quick to tell people what they should do. Quick to judge, slow to forgive. They believed in exact retribution for offenses. Forgiveness, on the other hand, expands like a Coke that has been shaken hard before being opened. It just goes everywhere, multiplying in running-over fashion. (See the sermonette on forgiveness in Luke 17:1–4.)

This section also defines the holy life. Similar to being merciful as the Father is merciful (6:36), we are also called in verse 40 to be like the teacher. Jesus is the best definition of Christianity. The New Testament defines holiness as

Christlikeness. This is especially true when it comes to our judgment of others, especially when we can't see them for the log hindering our own vision. This makes Jesus's rebuke and judgment of the religious leaders even more severe. Because his vision is unimpeded by logs, he sees them clearly and states honestly what he sees.

The log in the eye has become a common reference to self-knowledge. As followers of Jesus, we are given eyes to see clearly. This theme runs throughout the Gospel—the healing of the blind, opening of the eyes on the road to Emmaus (24:31), and in the little teaching in Luke 11:33–36, where Jesus calls the eye the lamp of the body. If the eyes are healthy, the whole body is healthy. If the eyes are sick, the whole body is sick. The church of Jesus would do well to listen carefully to these teachings. Repentance begins in the house of God as we tend first to our own darkness. Only as we see ourselves as Jesus sees us can we be made right to see the rest of the world as it really is. The log in our own eye is the greatest hindrance to loving our neighbor like God does.

Luke 6:43–45. This little illustration continues along the same path. The essence of a tree comes out in its fruit, even as the essence of the heart comes out in our words and deeds. Sooner or later, the real person shows up, for good or evil. A few times I have worked in situations where I suspected immorality. Rather than judging without proof or insinuating guilt, I waited. Patience allows people to reveal who they really are. The history of a person does not lie. And the only thing that can change the trajectory of history is an encounter with Jesus, the removal of a log in the eye, the fullness of mercy in the heart.

Luke 6:46–49. So what do we do in light of all this? We build our house on a solid foundation that will withstand the storms that are coming. We hear the words of Jesus and act on them.

GOING DEEPER

Read the Matthew account of the Sermon on the Mount side by side with the Luke account. What is left out? Is anything added? In what ways does Matthew's audience (primarily Jewish) shape the content? How does Luke's mission to the gentiles shape the text?

Discuss together how the same event can be faithfully told in different ways, depending on the audience. Some are bothered by these discrepancies in the Bible, but these different ways of telling the story actually do more to support its authority. God is breathing these stories into new communities through the human perspective of biblical writers, which gives us hope that God can do the same in our communities.

CONSIDER THIS

1. Name an enemy hard to love.

2. How many phrases in these texts have become common sayings? Have any of these lost their original meaning?

3. Why are humans most blind to their own sins/logs/specks?

4. In 6:49, Jesus talks about a great house falling. Might this be a hint at his declaration that the temple will be destroyed? If so, how does this text explain the fall of the temple as the center of religious faith?

11
WHEN MESSIAH ISN'T WHAT WE THOUGHT HE'D BE

SCRIPTURE

Luke 7:18–35

THE BIG IDEA

Identifying the Messiah is not easy. John the Baptist is introduced early in the Gospel as the prophet of the Most High who will go before the Lord to announce his coming (1:76–79). His ministry is likened to Isaiah in Luke 3:3–6. He prepares the way of the Lord. John is viewed as the last of the Old Testament prophets, and Jesus is viewed as the first of the new kingdom prophets (see Luke 23:62–65). But here, even John the Baptist expresses doubts that Jesus is the Messiah of God. Apparently, his expectations do not mesh with Jesus's ministry.

CORE TEACHING

We all have a little do-it-yourself Messiah shop in our imaginations. We have crafted from the raw material of our expectations a God who comes to us in specific ways. I suppose we are returning the favor to God. In the beginning, God made us in his image, and we are now making God in our image. Like the idol makers of Isaiah 44, we have cast God as we think God should be.

John the Baptist is no exception. He grew up in a culture ripe with messianic expectation. Most popular opinion agreed that the Messiah would be a political and/or military leader who, like King David, would overthrow enemies and liberate the land from pagan power and influence. Then Jerusalem could be the center of the world and dazzle the world with the wealth of its treasury, the strength of its army, and the holiness of its temple. The nations would stream to Mount Zion to worship such a Messiah.

John's earliest messages didn't seem to buy into this popular opinion, but now that he is imprisoned and hearing only bits and pieces of the news about Jesus, he sends his disciples with a question. "Are you the one who is to come, or should we expect someone else?" (7:20). I suppose if you were about to lose your head for prophesying the arrival of the Messiah, you'd want to make sure you had the right one too. I wonder what John was *not* seeing or hearing that gave him pause.

Jesus does not chide John in any way for the question. Rather, he offers this blessing: "Blessed is anyone who does not stumble on account of me" (v. 23). Given the opposition to Jesus throughout the Gospel, it *seems* that Jesus is blessing all those who have been offended by his ministry. That's a big parade. But that is not what is happening here. Jesus is speaking specifically about John. If he can take no offense that God is present when the blind receive their sight, the lame walk, the lepers are cleansed, the deaf hear, the dead are raised, and the poor have good news preached to them, then he is blessed. Jesus is defining for John the essence of the coming of the kingdom. Luke is writing for the early church, still living with political-messianic hopes. In the public ministry of Jesus, we have seen God. And, as it usually turns out, God is different than we thought God might be.

Jesus then speaks to the crowds about John and his greatness as a prophet—yea, more than a prophet. Yet, Jesus says, the least in the kingdom are greater than John. This includes even tax collectors, who have encountered Jesus's claim on their life. John's baptism unto repentance led them to believe in Jesus. But the rejection of John's baptism by the Pharisees and lawyers excludes them from the kingdom. Due to a log in their eye, they could not see beyond. Rather than removing the log, they accused John of having a speck in his eye. John rightly named the activity of God in the world. Those who saw believed, and were baptized.

After this, Jesus confronts the crowd because of their rejection of his mission. They had their minds made up about Messiah, and Jesus did not fit the description. Jesus likens them to children who won't dance when the music is played or join the game going on in the middle of the room. They sit sulking on the sidelines. They found fault with both John and Jesus.

GOING DEEPER

We don't define God. God will not take the shape of our desires; rather, God invites us to be invaded by his holy love, changed by his transforming power, and made like his Son, Jesus. Any god with any agenda, other than making us

Christlike, is most likely a handmade, homemade god. Be assured that these gods cannot save us. We might as well save ourselves as soon as depend on a self-constructed god.

Read Isaiah's caricature of handmade gods in Isaiah 44:9–20.

CONSIDER THIS

1. Why do you think John is questioning Jesus?

2. Read the preceding text, Luke 7:11–17. Jesus raises the dead son of a widow, and the response of the people is that "A great prophet has appeared among us!" (v. 16). How does the text that follows connect to this?

3. What are some of the homemade gods you have seen in your lifetime?

4. Why are tax collectors greater than John the Baptist?

HARD OF LISTENING

SCRIPTURE

Luke 8:4–15

THE BIG IDEA

    This is a story about the way the gospel goes into the world. It is important that we hear the parable because it is about both the seed *and* the soil. It rises out of the language in Isaiah, where a prophet is told to preach even though the people do not have ears to ear. In other words, immediate response is not our motivation to keep telling the story. The seed does its saving and judging work, even if we don't see it.

CORE TEACHING

    "Whoever has ears to hear, let them hear" (Luke 8:8). What a way to end a parable. Jesus punctuates his story about the sower with the challenge to listen. We find a similar challenge in the Revelation of Jesus to John, where each of the letters to the seven churches ends with, "Whoever has ears, let them hear what the Spirit says to the churches" (Revelation 2:7, 11, 17, 29; 3:6, 13, 22).

Ears have no other function. They certainly don't adorn our heads. I've never heard anyone complimented for having beautiful ears. Of course, it *would* be hard to keep glasses balanced on our noses without the aid of ears. If you have ears, *listen*.

Luke runs through the parable twice, but we would be wrong to assume he means the same thing both times. The first time through (vv. 4–8), the focus is on the confidence of the sower in the seed about the ability of the seed to do what seed is made to do—namely, grow. The sower flings seed everywhere. He doesn't aim it or place it in plowed rows or take care where it falls. He just thrusts his hand in the seed sack and comes up slinging seed in every direction. I suppose what Luke wants everyone to know is that Jesus spreads the good news of the gospel everywhere, without discrimination. Anyone with ears to hear can catch the seed.

When the disciples got Jesus alone, they asked him questions about the parable. It didn't make sense to them. Why wouldn't the sower be more careful with the precious seed? Why did it sprout some places and not in others? And why tell people parables they can't understand? Jesus answered, "The knowledge of the secrets of the kingdom of God has been given to you, but to others I speak in parables, so that, 'though seeing, they may not see; though hearing, they may not understand'" (v. 10). This convoluted answer only deepened their confusion.

Well, of course that makes perfect sense. You sling gospel seed at people by way of imperceptible, non-understandable parables so they won't get it and, in turn, won't ask to be forgiven. What kind of gospel is this? Some view this scripture, and Jesus's response to the disciples' question, as proof of divine election. Some have been chosen by God to hear, and others have not. I doubt this interpretation, however. Jesus in Luke's Gospel consistently opens the door for everyone, without any sense of some being excluded. The Gospel of Luke is about outsiders being invited in, not some being kept out. So what kind of gospel is this?

Apparently it's a gospel that reveals its reception in the hearer. Jesus explains the parable to the disciples in verses 11–15. This time, though, the focus is neither on the sower nor on the seed—but on the soil. The soil is the receptor of the seed, just as our ears are the receptors of the gospel. The gospel is preached everywhere, but it doesn't produce fruit in every life. Only in the lives of those whose ears/soil are good. Same seed, the same powerful, patented seed for everyone. The difference is in the ears.

Grandma won't take her medicine. You remind her and remind her, but she sits there like a bump on a log in the next county. "Huh?" she says, straining her neck in evidence that she hasn't heard you.

You get in her face and speak the words slowly, with extra volume. "Grandma. You. Have. To. Take. Your. Medicine."

The look on her face registers nothing. You repeat it, with more volume. Nothing.

But whisper a sarcastic comment two rooms away, and you'll get an immediate response from her. "I heard that!"

Grandma isn't hard of hearing. She is hard of listening.

GOING DEEPER

This story connects well with an earlier story in Luke 5, about the call of the disciples. In Luke, the good news is heralded by the angels at the birth of Jesus, he is called and blessed by God as the anointed Messiah, and he calls disciples to join him on the journey of God to all people—both Jews and gentiles. The new Israel—the twelve tribes now embodied in the disciples—begins to spread the good news of the kingdom of God. As you study the Gospel of Luke (and on into Acts), be sure to keep connecting the dots of the larger narrative.

Read Revelation 2–3. How are the seven churches challenged to hear?

CONSIDER THIS

1. Read the call of Isaiah in Isaiah 6. How are these two stories similar? How are they different?

2. Do you have friends who are characterized by the four soils described in Luke 8:12–15?

3. How do you cast the seed?

4. Is hard soil always hard, or can it change? Do thorns last a whole lifetime?

5. Discuss this statement: God has not called us to examine the soil but to sow the seed.

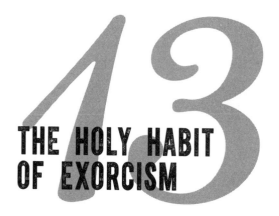

THE HOLY HABIT
OF EXORCISM

SCRIPTURE

Luke 8:22–39

THE BIG IDEA

The evil in our world is real. And Jesus goes right into the heart of it to free people from its destructive power.

CORE TEACHING

Read the headlines of your local newspaper. How is destructive power being used? When I read these kinds of things, it makes me want to run and hide. But that raises the question, "Who will face this evil?" I find myself thinking about a police officer who knocks on the door of domestic violence; the social worker who sits across the table from a child abuser; a teacher face to face with an angry student; an emergency room team treating rival gang members; a public defender in a cold courtroom; an undercover drug agent making a bust; the counselor of a client who has purchased a gun; a prison guard breaking up a fight with no one watching his back.

These people can't run. It's their job. They face daily evil in its rawest, deadliest forms. Have you ever wondered what Jesus might mean to these public servants? Study closely today's story from the Gospel of Luke.

The geography of the story is simple. The lake is in the middle. On one side of the lake is the safe, religious world of the Jews. The comfort zone. On the other side of the lake is the wild, threatening land of the gentiles. The chaos zone. The sea—the mythical home of the devil lies in the deep, blue sea—separates these two turfs.

En route from one side to the other, the devil brews a storm that scares seasoned sailors spitless. Sheer fear seizes them, so they wake Jesus. And Jesus rebukes the storm. When Jesus speaks, the storm stops.

It reminds me of my eighth-grade shop teacher, Mr. Craft. Don't you think that's a good name for a shop teacher? Mr. *Craft*. He'd walk in on thirty eighth graders horsing around with hammers, boards, and power tools. He'd say one word: "Boys!" And you could hear a pin drop.

I wonder what Jesus said to the storm. Probably not, "Boys!" Maybe just, "Shhhh!"

The disciples became as in awe of Jesus as they were of the storm. "Who is this?"

They were beginning to catch on that the Most High God had put on skin and crawled into their boat. But before they had time to figure it out, they arrived on the other side.

Gentile territory. Gang turf. Devil's ground. And a man in whom the devil had brewed a mess immediately greeted them. Townspeople had incarcerated him in chains, and he'd broken loose. He once lived in a house with his family. Now he lived in a graveyard, the abode of unclean bodies and spooks. He was wild, naked, uncontrollable, nasty, loud, and threatening—chock full of demons. Demons had separated him from his family, his home, his town, his friends, his clothes, his sanity, and his senses. And now demons had taken over his voice and were talking to Jesus.

When *The Exorcist* was re-released, a *Good Morning America* poll said that it was the scariest movie of all time. Something tells us that nothing is as frightening as what the devil can do, given free reign inside a human body.

The demons see Jesus and ask their fate. They suddenly become like eighth-grade boys in Mr. Craft's shop class. Jesus demands their name. They are legion, which means 5,600. We've met most of them in our lives. They have names. Rage. Anger. Envy. Violence. Prejudice. Abuse. Rape. Drugs. Alcohol. Wildness. Pornography. Murder. Theft. Madness. They all have names. And they do great harm. This man is their poster child. He is their apartment complex. He is their post-office box. I don't know about you, but if I'm one of the disciples, I'm backtracking toward that boat.

I love Luke's comic relief. The demons know they are about to be evicted, and they beg to go live in a herd of pigs nearby. They prefer the low-rent district of squealing, mud-wallowing pigs to "the abyss." Jesus lets them move into the pigs. Once there, they make a beeline to the lake, the abode of the devil in the deep blue sea. They are going home to Papa. But little do they know that Jesus just put Papa in his place on the way over.

Then we meet the townspeople. They never really cared about the guy. They just wanted him out of their hair. Chained or out in the cemetery, it didn't matter, as long as they didn't have to deal with him. It seems that government, at best, can only restrain and relocate evil. There are limits to our human efforts to corral evil. When the townspeople hear about the man and the pigs, they go out to see what's going on. The change is awesome. The wild man sits at Jesus's feet. The naked man is wearing clothes. The demented man is in his right mind. The destructive man is at peace. The chained man is calm and free.

And the townspeople say the same thing to Jesus that the demons said. "Please go away. Please leave us alone. We are managing fine as we are." They are more afraid of Jesus than they were of the wild man.

Had I been these townspeople, I hope I'd have said, *Jesus, would you come to our jail? There are some people I want you to meet. Jesus, would you mind spending a day at the Department of Child and Family Services? There are some angry men I'd like you to meet. Jesus, would you meet with a senior high student who keeps threatening to beat me up if I fail him in my class? Jesus, would you come with me on a drug bust?*

I think Jesus would have said, "Yes, yes, yes, and yes."

He goes with us into the storm of evil that threatens to sink our communities. He goes with us to deal with hostile, angry, hateful demons that have taken up residence inside our fellow humans. He goes with us to jails, courtrooms, crime scenes, emergency rooms, dark alleys, angry homes, drug busts, drunken brawls, protests, and activist marches. He goes with us to the ends of the earth. It's where he's always been going. And if we dare read ahead in Luke 9:1–2, we discover that it's where Jesus is *sending* us.

GOING DEEPER

There is a great, five-minute scene in the movie *Grand Canyon*. A man's car has broken down late at night in an urban area. He calls a tow truck whose driver arrives at the same time that a gang begins to harass him. The tow-truck operator and the gang leader have a discussion about their roles. The gang wants to be unhindered in robbing the driver. The tow-truck operator wants the gang to leave and let him do his job. The gang leader has a gun and makes the point that respect is gained only at the point of a gun. The operator of the tow truck speaks the pivotal line in the scene. "Man, it's not supposed to be this way."

How is evil destroying your personal world? Your family? Your city? Spend some time praying to the God who confronts evil. Also pray for police officers, social workers, AA leaders, hospital emergency room personnel, and anyone else you can think of whose work places them face to face with evil in its most blatant and violent forms. These servants provide safety and health for the community.

CONSIDER THIS

1. What demons remain in the world today?

2. What are the dominant demons in your community?

3. Where else in Scripture does the sea represent the dark chaos of evil in the world? Look in the Psalms and Job for Leviathan and in Revelation for the sea beasts.

4. When have the people of God been too timid in confronting evil?

14
SNEAKING A MIRACLE

SCRIPTURE

Luke 8:40–56

THE BIG IDEA

By contrasting two very different kinds of sick people in the same story, Luke shows us how Jesus deals with the cultural-religious dichotomy between the clean and the unclean.

CORE TEACHING

The people in this story who sought Jesus's help could not have been more different on the scale of religious purity.

Jairus was a leader of the synagogue, a man held in highest regard by the people. His ritual work placed him in rare air, the highest strata of social status. He would be valued in the shame-versus-honor system of society. This system was a totem-pole ranking that had to do with family of origin, wealth, position, work, physical health, and social associations. Failure in any of these could take you to the bottom rung quite rapidly. And his little daughter was sick. In fact, she was dying—and did die before Jesus would even have a chance to get to her. Jairus summoned Jesus to come to his home and heal her. They were on the way when the second person in the story interrupted the ambulance run.

The woman in the crowd had been hemorrhaging for twelve years. Since the day Jairus's daughter was born, this woman had been bleeding. We can probably safely assume she had exhausted her savings on cures from quacks, charlatans, and doctors—all to no avail. She was ritually unclean and publicly known as unclean. To touch her would be a violation of the holiness code. She could be found near the bottom of the social totem pole. She had several strikes against her—woman, bleeding, and probably separated from her family. And she did the unthinkable. She touched Jesus.

Luke gives us a twelve-year-old disease and a twelve-year-old child. Jesus is on the way to help the high-status, clean family when the unclean, low-status woman defiles him by her touch. She did not intend to get caught. Shuffling her way through the fast-moving crowd, she figured on getting close enough to lay a hand on Jesus without it being noticed. Then she would drop back in the crowd and make her way quietly home. Hopefully the bleeding would stop and she could show herself to the priest and turn over a new leaf of acceptance in society. If she could only sneak a miracle out of the healer, her life would be vastly different.

It almost worked. She followed her game plan perfectly, got close enough, reached out and touched Jesus, and then started to drop back. But the whole crowd came to a grinding halt as Jesus stopped in the middle of the road. She was stuck a few layers of humans behind Jesus, and no one was passing her. The crowd was confused. Wasn't there an emergency at the home of the synagogue leader's house? Hadn't Jairus said, "Please come quickly"? But Jesus stopped.

And then he asked the question that made her want to die on the spot. "Who touched me?" (v. 45). Like asking on a crowded subway, an airplane aisle, or while exiting a packed stadium, it was a nonsense question. Everybody had touched him. They were a mob of concerned humanity walking down the road at a brisk pace to help a high-status member of the community.

But this was different. Jesus said, "Someone touched me; I know that power has gone out from me" (v. 46). And then the sea of people began to divide, and she was exposed in the middle of the crowd. Before anyone could say a word, thoughts were probably flying: *What is this unclean woman doing in a crowd of people anyway? Doesn't she know she could defile us all? Oh my! She has contaminated the healer. Now he can't go to Jairus's home and heal his daughter. This ruins everything. She slowed down the procession. The little girl could die while we're standing in the street dealing with a woman who shouldn't even be here. She doesn't deserve the holy man's time. The gall of this woman to have touched a clean rabbi.*

She came, trembling, to the feet of Jesus and told her story. With each sentence the twelve-year disease was disappearing in the rearview mirror. And, with each sentence, the twelve-year-old girl was slipping away. Could someone hurry this up? Enough time spent on the low-status woman!

Yet Jesus listened and replied, "Daughter, your faith has healed you. Go in peace" (v. 48). Don't mistake these words. *Daughter*—member of the family, insider, closely related to me. *Go in peace*—communal wholeness and belonging, no longer fractured from the worshiping community, free to enter the worlds of commerce and relationships. Jesus is doing more than physically healing this woman. He is saving her in every way a person *can* be saved.

In the middle of his pronouncement, a messenger arrives from Jairus's home. "Too late. She's gone. Trouble the teacher no more." But Jesus is not done. He declares that the little girl is not dead, only sleeping. (*Sure.*) But Jesus promises them, "Just believe, and she will be healed" (v. 50).

Six people went into the house. The mother and father. Peter, John, and James. And Jesus. They laughed at his suggestion that she was only asleep. And why not? They could plainly see she was no longer breathing, no longer pink. Jesus took her hand and commanded her to get up. And, miraculously, breath returned to her as she arose from the dead. They fed her. And they all kept quiet about what had just happened.

Now isn't that a kicker. The healing out in the street that a woman *tried* to keep quiet was known all over town. She snuck her miracle and was found out. The healing at the synagogue ruler's house—that would normally have been front-page, messianic news—is top secret. Jesus's PR plan for the kingdom of God doesn't always make sense. Imagine that.

GOING DEEPER

The words *save* and *salvation* really grow wide in Luke's Gospel. They mean healing physical illnesses, casting out demons, raising the dead, forgiving sin, restoring people to community, and delivering people from the evil one. Sounds a lot like Mary's song from Luke 1.

These stories belong together. The tension between them is what Luke is showing us. Jesus came to seek and save the lost. Social categories don't matter much to Jesus. Apply this to the people you know who think they are least likely to experience the grace and mercy of God. Who knows? Maybe this is their day to sneak a miracle.

CONSIDER THIS

1. Is there any significance in the number twelve?

2. Jairus has no lines. We are *told* that he begs for healing, but we don't know what he says to Jesus. The woman speaks a lot. Why?

3. What are the boundary lines of clean and unclean today?

4. In what ways is our culture today an honor-versus-shame culture?

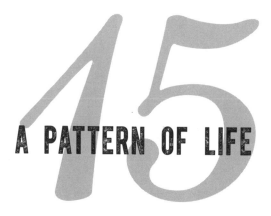

A PATTERN OF LIFE

SCRIPTURE

Luke 9:10–17

THE BIG IDEA

Several times in Luke's Gospel we find the formula "he took, he blessed, he broke, and he gave." This is what Jesus did with bread in the feeding of the five thousand and also at the Last Supper with his disciples in Luke 22:14–23. But it is more. What was done with bread is also done with Jesus. This formula finds its way into the sacrament of the Lord's Supper and, hopefully, into the life of the church as the pattern of Jesus's life.

CORE TEACHING

He took. The Father took Jesus into his love, laid claim to him in the womb of Mary as the holy child. Jesus was aware of his chosen-ness, his taken-ness, from early days.

His Father had work for him to do. Even as a child in Jerusalem sitting with the elders in the temple, he knew himself to be about his Father's business.

He blessed. The Father blessed Jesus. At his baptism the heavens opened, a dove came down and landed on him, and words of divine favor were spoken. The Father identified Jesus as his beloved Son, the *blessed* one. Under the power of this blessing, Jesus was able to move into the world, offering blessing to all. Never did being blessed become something that was all about him. He stood in the stream of the Father's abundant love and offered the living water to all who came to him thirsty.

He broke. Jesus was also broken by the Father. What was done to bread was done to Jesus. He was not shielded from the cruelty of a cursing world. He felt the pain of rejection, denial, betrayal, injustice, torture, and crucifixion. In the words of the religious sentiment of his day, "Cursed is the one who dies on a cross." Jesus went to the cross and died there in our place. What broke Jesus into pieces was his willingness to do the work of the Father in all the places where life was being taken from people. Brokenness is not something *in* the way. Brokenness *is* the way.

He gave. In the resurrection, the Father—who has taken Jesus, blessed Jesus, and broken Jesus—now gives Jesus away. His resurrected life is God's gift of blessing to all who believe in him. I find it interesting that Jesus does not pause for a victory lap at the mouth of the tomb, the site of Pilate's sealed warning. Had I been the script writer, I would have had Jesus standing on top of the rolled-away stone, delivering a message about who is really in charge of the world. Instead, we find an angel left behind with a message for the disciples. *If you want to follow him, he is already on the road to*

Galilee [where the work of God needs to be done]. We can go find him there if we are ready to get to work.

GOING DEEPER

Amy Sherman, in her book *Kingdom Calling: Vocational Stewardship for the Common Good,* suggests:

> Jesus' work is not exclusively about our individual salvation, but about the cosmic redemption and renewal of all things. It is not just about our reconciliation to a holy God—though that is the beautiful center of it. It is also about our reconciliation with one another and with creation itself. . . . This too-narrow gospel focuses believers missionally only on the work of soul winning. It has little to say about Jesus' holistic ministry or the comprehensive nature of his work of restoration. It focuses on the problem of personal sin only, thus intimating that sanctification is a matter only of personal morality (rather than that plus social justice). It focuses believers on getting a ticket to heaven, but doesn't say much about what their life in this world should look like. Put differently, it focuses only on what we've been saved from, rather than also telling us what we're saved for.[1]

If we rightly comprehend blessing, our vocation is much more than a career. It is the call of God to live in the awareness that we are chosen and treasured, beloved and blessed, broken and bruised—all for the purpose of being given away as the gift of God to others. Our vocation entails how we spend money, whom we have sex with, how we do our work, what kind of citizens we are, how we tend our lawns, and what our neighbors think of living beside us. The voca-

---

1. Amy Sherman, *Kingdom Calling: Vocational Stewardship for the Common Good* (Downers Grove, IL: InterVarsity Press, 2011), 67, 70–71.

tion we are called to requires awareness of the God who
called us to life and blessed us for the sake of others.

CONSIDER THIS

1. Recall your baptism. What does it mean to you today?

2. What is the difference between believers who live under
   the blessing of God and believers who experience God
   as a stern judge?

3. What difference does blessing make to us? For others?

4. What are the other texts in Luke where the taken,
   blessed, broken, and given formula appears?

WHO ARE THE PEOPLE
IN YOUR NEIGHBORHOOD?

SCRIPTURE

Luke 10:25–37

THE BIG IDEA

This is one of the most beloved parables of all. It is found only in Luke's Gospel. It defines the central theme of the Gospel: Jesus on mission to the world. The central question is the identity of the neighbor.

CORE TEACHING

Now that I have grandchildren, I have been reintroduced to the world of children's television. We watch *Sesame Street* together. I've been away for about fifteen years, but not much has changed. Elmo has gotten more popular. Big Bird is still nasally. The Count still loves to count things, "Ah, ha, ha!" Bert and Ernie are still at it. The humans on the show have aged a bit, but the puppets have all retained their youthful vigor. And they're still singing one of my favorite songs. "Oh, who are the people in your neighborhood, in your neighborhood, in your neighborhood? Oh, who are the people in your neighborhood, the people that you meet each day?" They are teaching children to feel safe in the confines of their own neighborhood, recognizing the people who come and go.

The next program is *Mister Rogers' Neighborhood*, now in syndication and transformed into *Daniel Tiger's Neighborhood*. People come and go in his little bungalow, and we feel safe among them. It's a very neighborly program.

I learned a few years ago that even cell phone companies are interested in neighbors. They let you add people to your cell phone neighborhood and communicate with them for less than it costs you to talk with strangers who live in another technology neighborhood. You are either in or out of someone's plan.

It should come as no surprise to us that the people of God are interested in neighbors because there was a time when they had none. They weren't on anybody's cell plan. No Egyptian or Babylonian children were running around singing, "Oh, an Israelite is a person in our neighborhood, in our neighborhood." They were strangers and aliens, outsiders in Egypt. They were being mistreated, and they cried out to God. God heard their cry and treated them in neighborly ways, bringing them out of slavery into a land flowing with milk and honey. Then he spoke to them in Deuteronomy 10:18–20. He told them to welcome the stranger because they had once been strangers and God loved them. They were to recollect their experience and be to others what no one had been to them.

Have you ever been a stranger? I recall my first trip to Moscow. The plane landed, and I carried all my belongings through a cement-walled hallway, past guards with automatic weapons and no smiles, to a booth where I was asked questions in a language I did not understand but in a mood I did. When I emerged from the checkpoints, I was supposed to be met by a host holding a card with my name on it. There was no host. I scanned the waiting area three times and saw no one holding up my name. So I sat down and waited. Fifteen minutes slowly turned into two hours. And there I was, sitting in an airport in Russia. I couldn't speak the language. I had no currency. I had no phone number to call, no address to take a cab to. And I remember feeling like an outsider.

In times like this, God seems to whisper. What I heard was, "Don't ever forget how you feel right now. This is how an unchurched person feels walking into a church. It's how a sick person feels waiting for test results. It's how a first grader feels in a new school. It's how a young couple feels in front of a marriage counselor. It's how a poor person feels asking for a job." God was telling me what God had told Israel. *Remember what it is like to be a stranger in a foreign place and to have no neighbor.*

And along came Jesus one day. A devout young scribe wanted to know what was required to inherit eternal life. Jesus replied in typical rabbinic fashion, answering a question with a question: "What is written in the Law? How do you read it?" (Luke 10:26). The young scribe repeated the Deuteronomy 10 answer. "Love God, love the neighbor." Rabbi Jesus awarded an A. "Do this, and you will live" (v. 28).

All was well until verse 29. "But he wanted to justify himself, so he asked Jesus, 'And who is my neighbor?'" The word *justify* is an accounting term. We justify our checkbooks to make sure we have exactly the amount we think we have. It is a *quantifying term.* The scribe wanted to *calculate* the meaning of neighbor. Here he was, a religious Jewish insider, standing inside his gated Jewish community, holding his in-plan cell phone, wanting to know how far this neighbor thing went. He was asking the *Sesame Street* question.

This time Jesus did not answer with a question. Instead, he told a parable. "A man was going down from Jerusalem to Jericho" (v. 30). That's all we get on the man. This is John Doe. We're not told if he is Jew, gentile, or neither. We don't know if he is rich or poor, white or black, heterosexual or homosexual, red state or blue state. But here, on this seventeen-mile stretch of dangerous road, he is beaten, robbed, and left half-dead in the ditch. What do we do with him?

We are given no clues to help us determine whether to stop. If he has a Bible in his backpack, we'd probably stop. Or a Christian bumper sticker on the rear of his dazed camel. Or an American flag patch on his jeans. Or a Trevecca Nazarene University sweatshirt. We're looking for clues that tell us we *should* stop. And we get nothing. He is a flat character, without lines, gestures, or facial expressions. In literature, he is called a foil. He reveals other characters by how they react to him.

Remember, the devout young scribe stood there with his question hanging in the air: "Who is my neighbor?"

You know the story. The priest came along, saw the guy, kept his distance, and went on by. The Levite came along, saw the guy, kept his distance, and went on by. I know the commentary explanations. They were holy men who did not want to defile themselves by touching an unclean man. It would have barred them from performing their religious duties on the Sabbath. Or it could be a trick and the guy in the ditch was playing possum while his thug buddies hid behind a rock waiting for some do-gooder to come over and check him out.

I don't know why they kept going. I suspect it has something to do with the fact that, if we keep our distance from needy people, don't look them in the eye, it is easier to walk on by. A hasty exit solves lots of obligations.

In Jesus's day, stories like this one usually had three responders to the foil. The first two were the villains, and the third one was the hero. We've had a priest and a Levite. Let's see, that leaves . . . a scribe. Our friend was waiting for Jesus to make him the hero of the story, given that he got an A on the first test.

Jesus continued, "But a Samaritan, as he traveled, came where the man was" (v. 33). You can almost hear the scribe's mental anguish. *A Samaritan! Gimme a break. A half-breed, theologically misguided, black-sheep, two-bit, redneck, pile-o-junk, worthless Samaritan?*

Luke has set us up to feel this way about Samaritans. A chapter earlier (Luke 9:51–56), Jesus and the disciples experienced remarkable inhospitality in Samaria. They had said they didn't take kindly to their being there. And here came one of 'them' into the parable.

The story slowed down as the Samaritan took great pains to go over, feel pity, bend down, pour disinfecting wine on wounds, and then rub oil over them to bring healing. He picked the man up, placed him on his animal, took him to the nearest inn, tended to him through the night, and left the innkeeper an open credit card for anything else the man might need.

I've been thinking about the difference between the first two travelers and the Samaritan, and I've concluded that they were looking for some signal of responsibility for the man in the ditch. They were looking for something they could easily see that would tell them he was a neighbor. The Samaritan looked, instead, into his own heart for something that told him he was responsible.

When the parable ended, Jesus had not answered the scribe's question. Instead, Jesus had changed the question from, "Who is my neighbor?" to "Which of the three was a neighbor?" I suppose that means that people in ditches get to quantify what *neighbor* means. And there are plenty of people in the ditches of the roads we frequent. And they are all asking the same question. *Who is my neighbor?*

I was wondering if I could give them your name.

GOING DEEPER

Substitute your own stories about being a stranger at some point in your life or tell the stories of strangers among you.

CONSIDER THIS

1. Why is this story so cherished across time?

2. Tell the story of your favorite Good Samaritan.

3. How does Luke 9:51–56 prepare us for the parable?

4. Read Acts 1:8 and 8:4–25. What has changed in the world of the disciples between Luke and Acts?

THE MOST CONSEQUENTIAL PRAYER

SCRIPTURE

Luke 11:1–4

THE BIG IDEA

The Lord's Prayer is the most memorized, most repeated prayer in the Christian faith. And rightly so. It is the prayer that Jesus taught us to pray. But familiarity often breeds contempt. Today's reflection is an attempt to recover the radical nature of the prayer for the Christian church.

CORE TEACHING

In the ninth grade, Jim Covington and I did a report on UFOs. We scoured the library, gathered the pictures, and read the testimonies of people who had seen them. In the process, we met an old guy who claimed to have been abducted by aliens. He was as convinced as gravity that they were all around us. "We can't see them," he'd say, "but they are here."

WiFi interests me as part of the same idea. It may be present in this very room, but we can't know by looking at the ceiling or under the chairs. It is here, but you only know it if you are able to access it and use it. It can be powerfully present, and you can be totally oblivious to it—but it is still here.

I'm fascinated by the idea of realities that may exist all around us while we remain completely unaware. I was confronted by such a reality in 1972 as a sophomore at Trevecca Nazarene University. Eli Stanley Jones spoke in chapel, and forty-plus years later, I am still captivated by what he had to say. He was in his eighties and writing a book on the same topic he spoke on that morning: *The Unshakable Kingdom and the Unchanging Person.* I still have my 1972 edition of the book. He came talking to us about the kingdom of God.

We don't preach much on the kingdom of God. Jesus did. And our people don't really have a clear understanding of the kingdom of God. For some of them, it is where we go immediately after we die. For others, it is what the religious right intends to establish on earth if they can secure enough money and votes. And for still others, it is securely stored in a heavenly vault, waiting for God to enter the secret, end-time code. I don't know. I think it might be a lot more like UFOs, if they are real, and WiFi, if it is present—already sitting among us, ready to launch.

In reading the Gospels, we discover that the kingdom of God is the primary message of Jesus. Jesus came to Galilee, proclaiming the good news and saying, "The time has arrived, the kingdom of God has come near; repent and believe the good news." This announcement is central to all that we believe. Jesus, in the mode of a prophet, believed that the time was ripe for God's exiles to come home, for

Israel to be delivered from its enemies, and for the justice of God to set things right. Because Israel's present course was way off track, divine judgment would be necessary. He would reconstitute the people of God around himself and inaugurate the kingdom of God.

Jesus said all kinds of things about the kingdom: It is among you. It will come in fullness, but make no mistake, it is already here. Repent, adopt another agenda, and enter it. Seek it first, and your worries will be quieted. It belongs to unlikely people: the meek, the poor, the persecuted. It begins small and insignificant, like a mustard seed. It is like a pearl of great price—worth every penny you pay. It is like a treasure hidden in a field—whatever it costs, go sign the deed. People who thought they could never get in are on the invitation list. Sometimes humble sinners are lots closer to it than buttoned-up churchgoers. Old wineskins can't hold it because it swells. It is like a party that the wrong people are invited to. When the sick are healed, it is here. When Satan is cast out, it is here. When forgiveness is freely given, it is here. When poor people resemble Jesus, it has arrived.

I have been thinking about our passion, what we church folk most want and need, what we actually ask God to do, what we pray for. When the first disciples asked Jesus to teach them to pray, he essentially said, "Pray this: Our Father in heaven, sanctify your name in us and among us. Your kingdom come, your will be done, on earth as it is in your heavenly kingdom" (see Matthew 6).

The kingdom of God is a realm, a reality, a sphere, an environment that is filled with the uncontested presence of God. In the words of the gospel, the kingdom of God has come among us in the person of Jesus Christ. He is here, and the kingdom is here in him. And this kingdom is wherever God's will is being done.

We get together often and pray this risky, crazy prayer that imagines the world we are living in made right by the in-breaking kingdom. I believe this is the most life-altering, radical, dangerous, consequential prayer we can pray: "Your kingdom come, your will be done on earth." Of course, I know we can say these words without meaning them, and not much happens, except we get more used to praying things we don't really mean. I think this is why so many liturgies calling us to pray the Lord's Prayer say, "Let us be ever so bold as to pray . . ." Let us be *bold*? Let us be *ever so* bold? Have you ever thought of yourself as needing boldness to pray for the kingdom to come? The Lord's Prayer is not a prayer for timid people. It is a prayer for the overturn of the powers that rule the world. It is a prayer of unsettling. It seeks more radical upheaval than the most radical terrorists you will ever find. It requires more devotion than the KKK or Hitler's regime or American democracy—or even SEC football. This prayer asks God to make his rule tangible everywhere, in every way, for this earth to become the place where God's will is done. We are inviting a tiger out of the cage. And this tiger is not tame.

Have you ever wondered what the world might be like one day if we prayed, "Your kingdom come" and God said, "Okay. I'll remove the barrier and let my kingdom come in all its fullness"? It would be like a dam breaking or a tsunami hitting land or a hurricane coming ashore—except everything in its path would be restored and made right. Can you imagine that? Can you pray for that? Wealth would be redistributed, and most of us would have less. The military would be unnecessary. Weapons would become farm implements. Washington, DC, would no longer be the seat of power. The meek would inherit the earth. The planet would be restored and redeemed from our pollution.

The weak among us would be empowered. The proud and arrogant among us would come down. Truth would be told everywhere. Power would be used to serve the neighbor. Justice would be done in the courts. Healthcare would be global, and the hungry would be fed. Education would not be for the privileged few but for everybody. Self-rule would cease, and God would be the only sovereign.

Because religious experience has become so narrowly individualistic, we need the kingdom of God to remind us that God has dibs on human tissue, economic theory, political philosophy, interpersonal relationships, power, work, play, entertainment, music, thought, athletics, and even graveyards.

So how does the kingdom come to earth? Look no further than Jesus. It comes in a body who—rather than turning stones into bread or making a deal with the devil for the kingdoms of the earth or proving himself by leaping from the pinnacle of the temple—empties himself in suffering love, takes up the cross, and dies in the very pits where our life is taken from us. The kingdom of God comes in suffering love to challenge the agenda of an old and dying world. We live in this world, but we are not of it. Not because we belong to a kingdom far, far away where we will go someday when we die, but because this is our Father's world, the battle is not done, Jesus who died will be satisfied, and earth and heaven will be one. We are the people who have come home from exile in Jesus. We are the new temple built upon Jesus. The body of Christ exists to receive and live out the kingdom of God. When we do God's will on earth, the kingdom has broken through in flesh and blood. We are kingdom boots on the ground at work in the redemption of all things.

When we pray "your kingdom come," do we really mean it? What makes the kingdom so radical is that, when God's kingdom comes, ours ends. It is the end of self-rule. God has not come to make some good suggestions or to lobby for his agenda. God has come to reign.

The day that Eli Stanley Jones preached on *The Unshakable Kingdom and the Unchanging Person*, I listened carefully. I knew I had heard truth. I made my way back to Smith Hall, knelt beside a bunk bed, and yielded all that I was to this Christ and this kingdom. It has cost me everything, and it has given me everything.

GOING DEEPER

I'm amazed by the characters in the Bible who actually knew how dangerous Jesus was: the Sanhedrin, King Herod, Pontius Pilate, Caesar, and Satan. They knew that the kingdom of God was the end of them. They didn't kill Jesus because they disagreed with his ideas; they killed him because he had come to destroy their little kingdoms and bring their rule to an end. They saw the kingdom of God as their end.

Barbara Brown Taylor tells the story of a loggerhead turtle. The turtle had made its way from the ocean to the beach to lay her eggs in a sand nest. After watching for a while, Taylor left, so as not to disturb the turtle. The next day, she noticed that the tracks of the turtle led not toward the ocean but into the blistering dunes. As she followed the tracks, she found the turtle exhausted and nearly baked. She found a park ranger with a Jeep and watched him set out to rescue the turtle. She writes,

> As I watched in horror, he flipped her over on her back, wrapped tire chains around her front legs, and hooked the chains to the trailer hitch on his Jeep. Then he took

off, yanking her body forward so fast that her open mouth filled with sand and then disappeared underneath her as her neck bent so far I feared it would break. The ranger hauled her over the dunes and down onto the beach; I followed the path that the prow of her shell cut in the sand. At ocean's edge, he unhooked her and turned her right side up again. She lay motionless in the surf as the water lapped at her body, washing the sand from her eyes and making her skin shine again. Then a particularly large wave broke over her, and she lifted her head slightly, moving her back legs as she did. As I watched, she revived. Every fresh wave brought her life back to her until one of them made her light enough to find a foothold and push off, back into the water that was her home.

Watching her swim slowly away and remembering her nightmare ride through the dunes, I noted that it is sometimes hard to tell whether you are being killed or saved by the hands that turn your life upside down.[1]

CONSIDER THIS

1. What is the kingdom of God? Where else do we find it mentioned in the Gospel of Luke?

2. In what ways is the kingdom already among us? How is it yet to come?

3. What will cause you to pray the Lord's Prayer with a new understanding?

1. Barbara Brown Taylor, "Preaching the Terrors," *Leadership Magazine* (Spring 1992), 44.

4. How would you describe your world if the kingdom came in fullness?

5. How much of this is possible now, through the obedience of God's people?

THE FINGER OF GOD

SCRIPTURE

Luke 11:14–36

THE BIG IDEA

The coming of the kingdom of God is the overthrow of dark powers. Some are able to see this in the ministry of Jesus while others critique him and ask for more signs.

CORE TEACHING

In the story of the Exodus, at one point the magicians of Pharaoh see the miraculous plagues and declare, "This is the finger of God" (Exodus 8:19). A little later in the story, God inscribes the Ten Commandments with his finger. Luke draws on these stories to point to a superior authority on site in this exorcism.

Luke writes more about the Holy Spirit and the exorcism of evil spirits than Matthew or Mark. We also see this

49

CLEAN OUTSIDE, DIRTY INSIDE

SCRIPTURE

Luke 11:37–12:12

THE BIG IDEA

Jesus attacks the Pharisees for their hypocrisy. Then he goes on to call his disciples to a fearless confession of faith before the very people he has just accused of being hypocritical.

CORE TEACHING

The Pharisees always take a beating in the Gospels. Their name has become synonymous with religious hypocrisy—and for good reason. They are as meticulous as the day is long about matters of nitpicking legalism while ignoring the love and justice of God. They count tiny seeds to tithe every tenth one while allowing a poor widow to lose all she has before an unjust judge. They major on minors.

They also love places of honor and position. The honor/shame society that is founded on their purity laws is a weight around the neck of the common person. While securing their places of honor, they establish laws that cause commoners to be dishonored, impure, and excluded.

They load people with burdens and refuse to lift a finger to ease them. A few verses earlier, it is the finger of God that relieves a man of a mute demon. The finger of God liberates him of a burden. Yet these religious leaders add to the weight by tucking their fingers tightly inside their sacred robes while their neighbor struggles under the weight of legal burden. And one more thing: they are guilty of killing the prophets who confronted them. They refused correction from the messengers of God. The Pharisees will soon kill another prophet who dared take them on.

However, the followers of Jesus are called to be done with hypocrisy and to make a fearless confession before these very hypocrites. Everything will eventually come to light. They should not fear these empty graves and shallow facades. The Father has numbered the hairs of their heads and sees them. The Son of Man stands ready to acknowledge them before the Father.

The ones who should be afraid are the Pharisees because, in rejecting the authority of Jesus, they are blaspheming the Spirit of God that indwells Jesus. When the disciples face the hypocrites, they will do well to remember who holds ultimate authority over their lives. If they do this, they will come out fine.

GOING DEEPER

Many take great interest in the sin of blasphemy against the Holy Spirit. It has been called the unpardonable sin, and I suppose it is—but not in the way that we think. As long as people identify the activity of God as the activity of the devil, they will not turn to God for help. If you think light is darkness and darkness light, how can you come into the light? Jesus is not saying that people *cannot* change; rather, he's saying that, until they see Jesus as the salvation of God, they will remain in darkness.

It is like being shot on the street and rushed to an emergency room. As the surgeon comes in to operate on you, you believe the surgeon is the same person who shot you. Would you allow someone whom you believe wants to kill you to operate on you? As long as we view Jesus as evil, we will not open ourselves to his saving operation. The unpardonable sin is thinking that God is in cahoots with the devil. As long as we believe this, we will not seek salvation. But we can change our mind about God, and God will save us.

CONSIDER THIS

1. What are the deeds of modern-day Pharisees?

2. In what ways are Christians often suspected of hypocrisy?

3. Jesus tells his followers not to fear those who can only kill the body. We are beginning to see more martyrdom in our lifetimes. How does Jesus's command inform our response?

4. What can we do differently from the Pharisees to make ourselves clean inside as well as out?

WORRYING AND WATCHING

SCRIPTURE

Luke 12:22–48

THE BIG IDEA

In these smaller instructional sections, Jesus instructs his disciples regarding worry and watchfulness.

CORE TEACHING

I take great comfort in knowing that the thing God says to us the most is, "Do not be afraid." It must mean the people of God are afraid a lot, or else there would be no reason for God to keep repeating this line.

For the disciples in Luke 12, it is clear to me why they would need to hear this. Jesus has been called Beelzebul, the Pharisees are plotting how to take him out, John the Baptist has lost his head to the executioner's ax, Samaritans won't even let the disciples stay overnight in one of their hotels, demons are screaming at them, and Jesus has just finished talking about those who have the authority to kill them. Then he reminds them not to be afraid because, like the sparrows that God never forgets, the numbered hairs on their heads are unforgettable to God. Then Jesus suggests that they sell all their goods and invest themselves in a kingdom that nobody can see. Who's afraid?

We are. Because this amazing journey of faith we are on is unsettling in every way. If it doesn't unnerve you, you might be in the wrong story.

GOING DEEPER

Texts like these usually warn us to be ready for the coming of Jesus, and I agree that we should be ready. But for which coming? The function of the Gospels is to convince listeners that, in Christ, God has come to save. Luke keeps finding stories about being ready: slaves with lamps awaiting the arrival of the bridegroom, faithful managers left in charge of the farm, and servants entrusted with talents. Could it be that these parables were for those who weren't ready for the *first* coming of the Christ?

Our present concerns about readiness for the coming of Christ focus on his second coming. In a time when we're busy with every imaginable thing and our to-do lists are longer than the hours in the day, it is hard to stay focused.

But what if the readiness texts call us to be ready for *every* coming of Christ? As the risen Lord, he is always showing up in places and ways we never expected. Maybe the text is about every coming of Christ—today, at the breakfast table, the gas station, and the office. Once we get used to seeing him, we'll always be looking for his coming.

CONSIDER THIS

1. Are you a worrier?

2. When (if ever) have you experienced a time when you heard God saying to you, "Do not be afraid"?

3. *Monsters, Inc.* is a popular animated movie about fear. Discuss the premise and storyline of the movie and what nuggets of truth might be found therein.

4. How does the thought of the coming of God make you more afraid or more hopeful?

DECIDING TIME

SCRIPTURE

Luke 12:49–13:30

THE BIG IDEA

As Jesus makes his way to Jerusalem, the language of Luke takes on a much more serious tone. In these smaller sections, the same point is driven home in multiple ways: Jesus brings the kingdom. It is costly to enter it. Now is the time for repentance.

CORE TEACHING

Luke 12:49–59. Through two images—fire and baptism—Luke reveals the need for decisive action. Both are crisis events that call for action. The baptism Jesus refers to for himself is the ordeal that awaits him in Jerusalem, often referred to as the passion of Christ. It is viewed as a decisive moment for the salvation of humankind. The image of fire conjures a judgment of purification. The world is about to be judged. This coming crisis will not allow us to remain as we are, on the sidelines, delaying a decision. We can no longer be like the spectators who debated the veracity of Jesus's divine authority and asked for a few more signs to confirm it. These people knew how to read the signs of a coming weather front (vv. 54–56). It was high time they read the signs of the coming kingdom and acted on it. A second illustration of decisiveness is found in verses 57–59. Rather than going to court and trusting your fate to a judge who may find you guilty, settle your issues now. Stop delaying decision. Get busy and make things right.

Luke 13:1–9. Two historical tragedies are noted, one caused by human evil, the other by natural evil: Pontius Pilate enacted bloody vengeance on Galileans worshiping in Jerusalem. And eighteen people died when a tower near the Pool of Siloam fell. The question is a common religious question. *Did this happen to them because they were evil?* We want to know whether our sins will bring heavy retribution down on us.

The answer is both yes and no. Yes, sin carries its own payload. No, God does not go looking for evil to do his work of judgment. The judgment of God is God's first saving act, not his punishment. Jesus refuses to be drawn into the argument but instead uses these tragedies to make the same point that was made earlier. Tragedy like this tells us that the time to repent is now. Don't wait and risk something tragic happening to you. Rather than try to explain *why* evil happens, we should align ourselves with the kingdom that has the power to free us from its bondage and resurrect its death.

The parable of the fruitless fig tree makes the same point. Rather than cutting it down now, give it another year—because the prophet is near, and they may repent of their sins and bear fruit in keeping with the arrival of the kingdom of God. God is patient—but the time is now.

Luke 13:10–17. This story of the disabled woman healed in the synagogue on the Sabbath seems to leave the current flow of thought—but then again, maybe not. We have already seen one synagogue leader, Jairus, express great faith in God—but not this one. He confronts Jesus for healing the disabled woman on Sabbath. In his mind, Jesus could have done this any of the other six days in the week. Jesus's response invokes the name of Satan one more time. This is a persistent theme in this section of the Gospel because the issue is authority. Only the stronger man can evict the weaker man. Jesus is presented as the stronger one. Satan has bound this daughter of Abraham for eighteen years. It is high time that she be set free.

The synagogue ruler said to wait for another day. Jesus says that the kingdom is present, so let's set her free now. It is one more story of the urgency that Jesus's ministry brings to the towns and villages.

Luke 13:18–21. Two brief parables also seem to be off the beaten path of immediacy. But maybe not. In each act, someone does something small. A man plants a mustard seed. A woman adds yeast to the flour. Both are small acts that bear large results. Small acts. Huge consequences. A lot like a disabled woman healed on the Sabbath.

On the surface, this isn't big news, but for those with eyes to see and ears to hear, it is a sign that the kingdom of Satan is crumbling right before their very eyes. And the kingdom of God is being introduced through the ministry of Jesus. The choice to follow Jesus may seem like one small decision, but it changes the trajectory of a life, a family, a city, a world.

GOING DEEPER

Luke 13:22–30. The question is now asked, "Will only a few be saved?" After all the rejection and opposition we have seen to Jesus's ministry and the steep cost of being a disciple, just how many are going to sign up for this gig?

It's a fair question. And Jesus responds with a direct answer: The door is narrow. The masses don't saunter in to pique their curiosity or to take a casual look around. But for now, this narrow door is wide open to all who wish to enter. One day, that will not be so. A day of reckoning for what we have done with Jesus will come to our world, and then it will be too late to go bang on the closed door. The excuse of knowing about Jesus will not suffice at the fullness of the coming of the Lord. So one more time, Luke says, decide now, while Jesus is here and while the door is still open.

CONSIDER THIS

1. Have you known situations where a decision to follow Jesus has divided a family?

2. Why does Jesus not answer their question in 13:23–24?

3. Note the use of parables between stories in Luke. He is more intentional about highlighting the meaning of a story with an accompanying parable than the other Gospels are. How do these parables connect with the stories?

GUESS WHO'S COMING TO DINNER?

SCRIPTURE

Luke 14

THE BIG IDEA

The gospel of Jesus is a gospel of welcome. The dinner table is a common site of this new kingdom hospitality. We see the invitation in the parable of the great banquet.

CORE TEACHING

Of all the places habits can be observed, the dinner table may be the most revealing. Eating is all about habits. Where we sit. Saying grace. Pass the salt, please. Using the correct fork. Smacking our lips. Interrupting. Lecturing. Placing a napkin in our lap. Eating reveals habits.

In Luke's Gospel, Jesus came strolling into a world made new by his presence. He saw things differently. He behaved differently. His habits shattered the prevailing culture. He practiced habits rarely seen. And of all the possible places to introduce new habits, Jesus chose the table. Julia Child wouldn't have done what he did. Gloria Vanderbilt wouldn't have done what he did. The truth is, *we* are very hesitant to do what he did.

What exactly did he do? Well, to understand that, I'll need to tell you a little about meals and tables in Luke's day. There were four rules.

1. Meals were the way you managed the boundaries of your life. On normal days, your family gathered at your table. On special occasions you might extend the boundary to include others. Via meal invitations, you declared who belonged and who didn't. Rule # 1 sounds familiar, doesn't it?

2. Where you sat at a meal ranked you socially. As a guest, the closer you sat to the host, the higher your status. The further you sat from the host, the lower your status. You could tell the pecking order of the community by observing the seating pattern. Rule # 2 isn't so strange to us either, is it? I remember hearing one of our daughters arranging the seating for her birthday party. Best friends near, barely invited friends down at the other end of the table. And who among us doesn't try to arrive early at open-seating banquets? We don't want to get stuck eating with unimportant people all evening.

3. Meals were meant to be reciprocated. If you invited me, I'd be obligated to return the favor. It wasn't a courtesy; it was a must. So this means that I would be very careful about accepting an invitation because, after all, do I really want to reciprocate?

4. You only invited people who could affirm or improve your social standing. Your A-list included people who were higher than you in social standing. It took courage to invite

them because they might refuse your invitation due to the obligation to invite you back. Your B-list included people who were on your level. They were a safe ask. Your C-list was comprised of people you wouldn't think of inviting. They would drag you down.

It would be easy for us today to throw rocks at these rules, but this is just how it was. People were picky about table guests. People preferred the better seats. People excused themselves from invitations that obligated them. People thought of each other in pecking-order fashion. Into that world, Jesus came teaching:

> On one occasion when Jesus was going to the house of a leader of the Pharisees to eat a meal on the sabbath, they were watching him closely. Just then, in front of him, there was a man who had dropsy. And Jesus asked the lawyers and Pharisees, "Is it lawful to cure people on the sabbath, or not?" But they were silent. So Jesus took him and healed him, and sent him away. Then he said to them, "If one of you has a child or an ox that has fallen into a well, will you not immediately pull it out on a sabbath day?" And they could not reply to this.
>
> Luke 14:1–6, NRSV

Apparently Jesus had taught in the synagogue on Sabbath. He was a visitor en route to Jerusalem. The leading Pharisee thought him worth the risk of a dinner invitation. But, since he was the new guy, the Pharisees were watching him closely. On the way to dinner, Jesus came face to face with a bloated man whose body was retaining too much fluid. The curse of dropsy (which we know today as edema) is an insatiable craving for water coupled with the inability to void the water. This guy was killing himself with fluid, and his body was screaming for more. He craved the very thing he already had too much of. Jesus asked permission to heal him. The dinner party was dumbfounded. Not a word of reply. Jesus healed him and sent him home, explaining that they would have done the same for a cow or a child. Again, no reply. But I'm guessing they were thinking bad things about their dinner guest.

When he noticed how the guests chose the places of honor, he told them a parable. "When you are invited by someone to a wedding banquet, do not sit down at the place of honor, in case someone more distinguished than you has been invited by your host; and the host who invited both of you may come and say to you, 'Give this person your place,' and then in disgrace you would start to take the lowest place. But when you are invited, go and sit down at the lowest place, so that when your host comes, he may say to you, 'Friend, move up higher'; then you will be honored in the presence of all who sit at the table with you. For all who exalt themselves will be humbled, and those who humble themselves will be exalted."

Luke 14:7–11, NRSV

They had been watching Jesus to see what he would do. Now Jesus watched them scramble for the best seats in the house. They probably reminded Jesus of the bloated man: an insatiable thirst for what they already had plenty of. They were bloated with status and didn't know how to void themselves of it. Their bodies screamed for more. They wanted the seat of honor worse than the sick man had wanted a drink. Jesus, an equal-opportunity healer, offered a cure: Take the worst seat in the house. Instead of testing the pecking order, take the risk of humility. Accept your status as a gift from the host. Hope that the host will call you up.

All through Luke's Gospel, God does this—calls people up. From low to high. From down to up. From last to first. Jesus suggested a new dining habit. Rather than vie for status, receive it as the free gift of God. If you are thinking about saying "Amen" right here, think twice. Are we really ready to embrace this habit? We compete with each other for place and position. Not everyone stands on the medal podium at the Olympics. Only one person will be elected president. Not everyone gets promoted. There are bell curves. GPAs separate us. At graduation there are three kinds of *laudes*. In tournaments, you hope for first, second, or third place. Miss America is chosen from fifty, then from ten, then from five, and nobody remembers the runner-up. We have income brackets and social standings. You don't get far in this world by willingly taking last place.

What Jesus was suggesting to the Pharisees—and what he still suggests to us today—is social suicide. Jesus is out of step with the way our culture operates. His table habit would make everyone in their right mind think he had lost his.

But then, could this really cure dropsy? Could it cure the thirst for status that bloats us? Could we survive by receiving honor as a gift rather than wrenching it from each other? It's worth a thought.

As our text continues, you'll see that Jesus is also an equal-opportunity offender. Having addressed the guests about their game of power musical chairs, he turned to the host to talk about the guest list.

> He said also to the one who had invited him, "When you give a luncheon or a dinner, do not invite your friends or your brothers or your relatives or rich neighbors, in case they may invite you in return, and you would be repaid. But when you give a banquet, invite the poor, the crippled, the lame, and the blind. And you

will be blessed, because they cannot repay you, for you will be repaid at the resurrection of the righteous."
Luke 14:12–14, NRSV

Have you ever had the audacity to tell your host that they invited the wrong people to dinner? Jesus suggests to the host that he scrap his A-list, his B-list, his C-list, and go straight to his Z-list. The Z-list doesn't even exist in the host's imagination. The poor, disabled, lame, and blind aren't on anyone's list. They can't add to your status. They cost you points. They can't pay you back. Inviting them would be pure mercy.

GOING DEEPER

Our world doesn't work the way Jesus suggests it should. Financial planners don't work a crowd of bums. College professors don't have coffee with high school dropouts. Coaches don't frequent hospitals looking for recruits. Graduating college students don't list jobless people as references. Pastors don't usually inquire about an opening at a small church full of needy people. Doctors don't open a practice in a blighted area of town. Instead, we connect with people who can help us. We rarely open the boundaries of our lives to people who have absolutely nothing to contribute to who we are. This habit would go unrewarded everywhere in the world—with the exception of the resurrection of the righteous.

Apparently, one of the dinner guests wanted to change the drift of the conversation. Jesus's talk about a resurrection of the righteous reminded him of a saying.

One of the dinner guests, on hearing this, said to him, "Blessed is anyone who will eat bread in the kingdom of God!" Then Jesus said to him, "Someone gave a great dinner and invited many. At the time for the dinner he sent his slave to say to those who had been invited, 'Come, for everything is ready now.' But they all alike began to make excuses. The first said to him, 'I have bought a piece of land, and I must go out and see it; please accept my regrets.' Another said, 'I have bought five yoke of oxen, and I am going to try them out; please accept my regrets.' Another said, 'I have just been married, and therefore I cannot come.' So the slave returned and reported this to his master. Then the owner of the house became angry and said to the slave, 'Go out at once into the streets and lanes of the town and bring in the poor, the crippled, the blind, and the lame.' And the slave said, 'Sir, what you ordered has been done, and there is still room.' Then the master said to the slave, 'Go out into the roads and lanes, and compel people to come in, so that my house may be filled. For I tell you, none of those who were invited will taste my dinner.'"

Luke 14:15–24, NRSV

The unthinkable happened. An important man sent out invitations for a great dinner, and all the guests excused themselves. This was a social disaster. With each negative RSVP, his status stock plummeted. The invitees were wrenching from the host his standing in the community. It was social assassination. What was the host to do? He tried out Jesus's new dinner habits. Invited the Z-list: the poor, the disabled, the lame, the blind. But they wouldn't come on their own. They'd have to be convinced they were invited. They wouldn't believe their ears. They'd think it was a cruel joke and that they were being set up for a shaming. You'd have to compel them because they'd know they couldn't reciprocate the invitation.

What's that? There's *still* room at the table?

CONSIDER THIS

1. Often in the Gospels, the kingdom of God comes as a challenge to the existing cultural practices. How is that apparent in this text?

2. Name the last ten guests you dined with. Are they A- or Z-list people?

3. Who would be amazed to be invited to share a meal in your home?

4. How might our dining choices become our witness to Christ in the world?

23

WHICH OF THESE THREE IS NOT LIKE THE OTHERS?

SCRIPTURE

Luke 15

THE BIG IDEA

Jesus comes to seek and save the lost.

CORE TEACHING

The three parables of Luke 15 are all conditioned on one complaint. The scribes and Pharisees grumbled about Jesus eating with sinners. In their words, "This man welcomes sinners and eats with them" (v. 2). The inclusion of the excluded caused them to grumble and be in a foul mood. We are a long way at this point from the end of the third parable, but this is exactly where we need to connect the dots. The chapter is bookended by scribes and Pharisees grumbling that Jesus ate with sinners and a grumbling elder brother who could not believe that the waiting father offered such grace and forgiveness to the Prodigal Son.

Everyone else in the three parables rejoiced: the one who found the lost sheep along with his friends and neighbors; the woman who found the lost coin along with her friends and neighbors; and the father whose lost son came home along with the whole community. The only outliers in these stories were the scribes, the Pharisees, and the elder brother. They, therefore, are the focal point of the parables.

Listen to the exchange between the father and the elder brother and place the same words in the mouths of the religious leaders and Jesus. Imagine the religious leaders saying to God, "Listen! For all these years I have been working like a slave for you, and I have never disobeyed your command; yet you have never given me even a young goat so that I might celebrate with my friends. But when this son of yours came back, who has devoured your property with prostitutes, you killed the fatted calf for him!" (vv. 29–30, NRSV).

And then imagine the Father replying to them, "You are always with me, and all that is mine is yours. But we had to celebrate and rejoice, because this brother of yours was dead and has come to life; he was lost and has been found" (vv. 31–32, NRSV).

Several problems are to be noted here.

- The elder brother was not capable of compassion for "this son of yours." He no longer considered him as part of the family. The religious leaders excluded many of their own family—tax collectors, prostitutes, lepers, not to mention the gentiles. They were like the Levite and priest in the parable of the good Samaritan; they had learned to walk on by the people in the ditch.

- They were not grateful for the covenant that had been entrusted to them. They did not even understand that God had blessed them as keepers of his truth, his law, his mission. The blessings of being the covenant people were held selfishly. The elder brother wanted his fatted calf for a celebration with his friends. I'm guessing the guest list for this celebration would be quite narrow.
- Israel had lost the capacity to celebrate the activity of God. These were the same people who celebrated their deliverance from Egypt when the slaves came into the promised land. These were the same people who celebrated the return from Babylonian exile with trees clapping hands and mountains dancing. These were the same people who sang festal psalms of ascent as they marched to the temple to celebrate the coming of the messianic King. In Jesus, this was all happening in their lifetime, and all they knew to do was grumble that the lost were being found and the dead being raised.

It is a sad, sad day in the house of God when we are better at grumbling about sinners than we are about celebrating their return.

GOING DEEPER

Sometimes we break these parables into separate stories, but this chapter in particular is stronger and more hard-hitting if we study it all together. The connection of the grumbling at the beginning and the protest of the elder brother at the end is the main idea. The flow is simple. Sheep lost, searched for, found; everyone rejoices. Coin lost, searched for, found; everyone rejoices. Son lost, longed for, found; everyone rejoices—except the elder brother. Keep the spotlight there.

The searchers in these parables are the image of Jesus and the Father—the Good Shepherd who is not content with ninety-nine in the fold, the woman who searches carefully to recover the tithe, and the waiting father who longs for the return of the prodigal, knowing it cannot be coerced.

CONSIDER THIS

1. How lost were you? Why did you come home?

2. Which parable most resembles your story: someone who came looking for you, someone who was diligent until you were found, or someone who waited faithfully while you lived far away until things got bad enough for you to realize that this was no way to live?

3. Why has the story of the Prodigal Son captured the imaginations of artists and storytellers across the centuries?

4. Whom is God looking for through you?

LESSONS FROM A CROOK

SCRIPTURE

Luke 16:1–18

THE BIG IDEA

Given the messianic crisis in Luke, the wise steward will find his way into the future of the kingdom rather than doing the customary thing that most religious folk of the day were doing.

CORE TEACHING

This is one of those texts that most of us skip. It is hard to get our minds around Jesus making a hero of a dishonest manager. In other parables about masters and stewards, we find Jesus calling for faithful use of what belongs to the master, wise investment of talents, and watchful stewardship over the farm. Here, we have a master getting ready to fire a manager for squandering his assets. The unscrupulous manager becomes even more unscrupulous and curries favor with other potential employers by cheating his master out of what is rightfully owed. And Jesus holds this up as an example of what his disciples should do. I'm tempted to say, "Good luck. You're on your own!" Buy maybe there is something good here.

Do not minimize how bad this act is. Paint the manager as dark as your crayons will allow. It is actually in the stark contrast that the point of the parable emerges. Given the approaching crisis (he is about to be terminated, and his future is in jeopardy), the manager reads the time correctly and does the unorthodox thing. He acts in a way that seems wrong to everybody but may just assure him of a job in the future.

Here are the salient applications:

- This man reads the future better than the religious leaders of Jesus's day and knows how to find his way into it.
- The people who are embracing the kingdom at the cost of being ostracized by religious leaders may actually be making friends with the God of the future kingdom.
- Doing the unorthodox thing may get you kingdom currency.
- We are in the middle of a crisis regarding our future. Are we as wise as the world is shrewd about addressing it?

GOING DEEPER

Similarly to the parable about the widow and the unjust judge in Luke 18:1, Jesus at times uses anti-parables—stories about what not to do—that actually help us know what *to* do. Where else in Scripture are anti-parables used to make a point? Have you ever learned deep truth by observing unscrupulous behavior?

CONSIDER THIS

1. Why might Jesus use this odd way to teach a lesson?

2. What other lessons are there to be learned from the children of darkness?

3. Browse the rest of the Gospel of Luke for his use of money to talk about the kingdom of God.

THE OTHER NINE

SCRIPTURE

Luke 17:11–19

THE BIG IDEA

This is another of Luke's crossing-the-boundary stories. This one has to do with gratitude for inclusion in the kingdom.

CORE TEACHING

They were on the way to Jerusalem, traveling in the border territory between Galilee and Samaria. They had crossed the border at the end of an exhausting day of ministry. Sitting around the fire eating their sandwiches, Jesus and Levi were recapping the day. Levi leaned toward Jesus and said, "Nice trilogy. Lost coin, lost sheep, lost son. That was good. Especially the way you tied together the rejoicing of everybody except the elder brother. You think the scribes and Pharisees got the point?"

Jesus replied, "I suppose if they had ears to hear."

"We're really coming together as a team, aren't we? The twelve of us? Symmetry and all. I can't wait to get to Jerusalem. The news of what we are doing out here is really spreading fast. I think they'll be waiting. Do you think something big will happen in Jerusalem when we arrive?"

"Yes, I'd say something pretty big."

"Where are we headed tomorrow?"

"Samaria."

"I hate Samaria. Remember the welcome we got there last time? We set up our tent, handed out fliers, and nobody came. They wouldn't rent us a hotel room or let us eat at the local diner. I loved it when Peter pulled out his scorcher sermon on the last night and gave them the heat with "Sinners in the Hands of an Angry God." The Sons of Thunder were on a roll calling down fire from heaven to deep-fry the whole town. And then you stopped us!"

"There was a reason."

The next day found the traveling entourage in one of the border towns where ethnic tension always simmered just beneath the surface. As they entered the village, ten lepers approached. These people made your skin crawl. They were reduced to undignified dependence on frightened travelers. They came within the safe legal distance and began to yell out for mercy from Jesus and his friends. Apparently word of their arrival had preceded them.

Jesus instructed them to go and show themselves to the local priest to certify that they had been healed. If they passed this inspection, they'd be cleared to re-enter society. They could go back to their family, their work, and their synagogue. They turned and left, headed back toward the village from which they had come. Jesus and the Twelve followed them at a distance. But the ten were faster because they had important business with the priest.

Levi remarked, "Poor lepers. What an awful way to go. To be black-balled from society is a rotten way to live. What's going to happen to those guys?"

"That remains to be seen, Levi."

A few minutes later a fast-moving blur came streaking toward them at warp speed. He was bouncing up and down like a pogo stick. The guy was ecstatic! You could hear him coming. "Thank you, Jesus! Praise be to God! Hallelujah to the highest heavens! Hot diggity dog!"

It was one of the lepers. As the ten had made their way to the priest, they looked down at their arms and hands. Their skin was clean. Wholly clean. *Clean* clean. A skin-deep miracle had occurred. Nine of them kept bee-lining it toward the synagogue to get that priest's approval. But this tenth one stopped in his tracks, did an about-face, and headed back toward the site of his healing. As he approached, the Twelve backed away, unsure of his contagion. Jesus met him chest to chest as he leapt into the arms of the one who had proclaimed him clean. He couldn't stop thanking Jesus.

Grace had penetrated deeper than the leprosy. Giving thanks trumped getting an official clean bill of health. Something about the man betrayed his ethnic origin. The disciples began to whisper to each other, "Samaritan. He's a Samaritan."

Jesus heard the whispers and looked from the clean-skinned face into the travel-weary faces of the Twelve. "Were not ten made clean? The other nine—where are they? And why is it that this Samaritan—this outsider, this leper—is the only one to return and praise God for his healing?"

Nobody answered. How can you explain why outsiders are more grateful for healing than insiders? How can you explain why sinners praise more naturally than saints?

Jesus looked at the man and said, "Be on your way, my friend—to your family, your work, your synagogue. You are clean, skin and heart. Your faith has saved you."

Later that night Jesus and Levi were relaxing when Levi popped the question. "What did you expect us to say? How should we know where the other nine were?"

Jesus sat in silence for a minute before replying, "Levi, I just want you to remember that I crossed a border to find you too. Tax collectors have not been welcomed among the people of God—until now. So tell me, where is *your* gratitude?"

GOING DEEPER

In this narrative, the character of Levi is informed by Luke 5:27–32. Go back and read this text. How can these connections be made? Which other disciples could have filled the role of Levi in this imagined narrative? If you placed yourself in the role of Levi, how would the conversation between you and Jesus go?

CONSIDER THIS

1. How are the two borders similar: the exclusion of tax collectors and the prejudice against Samaritans? How are they different?

2. Where are the borders today?

3. What do you think the other nine lepers did? Whom do they represent in Luke's Gospel?

4. What borders did Jesus cross to save you, and when was the last time you thanked him?

THE OTHER NINE

133

BENCHMARKING RIGHTEOUSNESS

SCRIPTURE

Luke 18:9–14

THE BIG IDEA

The Pharisee and tax collector pray radically different prayers and receive surprising responses from God. The central idea is how we measure ourselves spiritually.

CORE TEACHING

Two men stand to pray in the temple. They lead radically different lifestyles. The Pharisee is every bit as good as he says he is in his prayer. And the tax collector is every bit as evil as the Pharisee says he is. But the tax collector is the one who goes home justified. Why? Because the Pharisee recognizes the gap between himself and the tax collector and offers the difference to God. The tax collector, on the other hand, recognizes the gap between himself and God—and asks for mercy.

In the Gospels we see that Jesus is very observant. He sees the world around him with eyes opened to what God might see. He sees what others walk past:

- A fig tree not bearing fruit
- A sower throwing seed where it has no chance of growing
- A widow putting a coin in the temple treasury
- A father waiting on the front porch for a wayward boy
- Hypocrites praying on street corners with one eye on a watching crowd
- Children being coldly dismissed by busy adults

Jesus moves in our world with the discerning eyes of God. But he focuses on *people*. He notices their speech, movements, gestures, postures, status, and body language. And he takes a second look to discern their stories. Jesus looks until he sees beneath the surface. That is what happens in the story of the Pharisee and the tax collector.

GOING DEEPER

Many theologies across the centuries have defined *holiness* as how we look: the clothes, makeup, and accessories we wear, the cars we drive, the houses we buy, and so on. Such a focus tends to keep me looking at me, concerned about how I appear in the eyes of others. I am the center of my own attention as I attempt to look holy. In this way of thinking, being a faithful witness means that I will place major emphasis on how I appear to others.

But what if appearance, though significant, is not meant to be the primary concern of a holy person? What if holiness is not so much how I look as it is how I *see*? Jesus seems to be non-self-conscious. We find little, if any, concern on his part about how others see him. He isn't invested in projecting a certain image. He doesn't look to see if others are watching him, and he doesn't adjust his behavior when he knows they are watching. He just sees the people in front of him and discerns the activity of God in their lives at a given moment. He sees what others fail to notice:

- A short man named Zacchaeus perched up in a sycamore tree
- A shy, bleeding woman whose grazing touch registered with him, even in a crowd
- A thief dying to his right
- A tax collector seeking mercy

Could it be that the holy life is more about how we see than about how we look?

CONSIDER THIS

1. The heroes in the Gospel of Luke are not the usual suspects. How is this still true in the church today?

2. How will final judgment reveal the people of God?

3. Given a choice, would you rather have the Pharisee or the tax collector as a next-door neighbor? Why?

4. Who is the tax collector among you today?

5. Who is the Pharisee?

27

THE STEEP COST OF FOLLOWING JESUS

SCRIPTURE

Luke 18:15–34

THE BIG IDEA

It is difficult for those whose security is rooted in wealth to follow Jesus.

CORE TEACHING

Luke 18 begins with the parable of the widow and the unjust judge. She is the model of the persistent, praying faith that the Son of Man hopes to find on the earth. Such faith is then seen in the prayer of the tax collector in verse 13 and then in the children of verses 15–17. We have been introduced to models of receiving the kingdom: a needy widow in prayer, a needy tax collector at temple, and a child who receives the kingdom as a gift. We have also seen the other side of the fence: a judge who does not fear God nor respect humans and won't give justice, a Pharisee who considers himself more righteous than the scoundrel tax collector, and the disciples who play crowd control and keep the children away.

Our introduction to the rich ruler is intended to place us in the crosshairs of decision. The story is told in a way that causes us to identify with him. We have kept the same commandments. We have followed the rituals. Then comes the deal breaker: "Sell everything you have and give to the poor, and you will have treasure in heaven. Then come, follow me" (v. 22). Have you ever known anyone to actually do this? Other than the monks of monasteries, some saints of olden times, and Catholic priests who take a vow of poverty? Who does this?

Our temptation is to soften the command. We spiritualize it. We explain ourselves out of obeying it. We emasculate the story of any real meaning. But what if this kind of obedience is exactly how the kingdom comes? What if we *actually* sell possessions and give the money to the poor? Would they believe the kingdom of mercy had landed on their doorstep or in their cardboard-box home?

Whatever you do with this, don't leave with nothing to do.

GOING DEEPER

This text might best be understood in tandem with the whole chapter. The connections flow from one story into the next. It is not without thought that Luke leads us immediately out of the call to costly discipleship and into the conversation with Peter. Where the ruler said no, Peter has left his nets and followed.

What do these disciples get for their sacrifice? "Many times as much," Jesus says (v. 30). But while they are estimating how much "many times as much" might be, Jesus announces for the third and final time that they are going to Jerusalem for a mocking, a flogging, and a killing. But on the third day, he will rise. But they do not understand anything he says.

CONSIDER THIS

1. Each story in this chapter has people who do not comprehend the kingdom. Who are they, and what is it about the kingdom that they do not get?

2. Why did the rich ruler go away sad?

3. In what way does money complicate following Jesus?

4. Do you believe Jesus intends that we live with no security, no insurance, no savings, and/or no retirement? At what point does our earthly security nullify our heavenly security?

28

LET THE WALLS COME DOWN

SCRIPTURE

Luke 19:1–10

THE BIG IDEA

Where God goes, the walls of Jericho keep crumbling as the gospel reverses fortunes, gives sight to the blind, and brings crusty characters to repentance.

CORE TEACHING

We have just moved from the outskirts of Jericho, where a blind man received mercy plus eyesight from the Son of David. Allow the imagery of Jericho in the Old Testament to inform your imagination. It was a place of formidable resistance to the people of God on their journey to the promised land. And here we have Jesus en route to the throne via the cross. Barriers stand in his way: the blindness of his disciples, the unwillingness of rich rulers to sell their possessions, the unwillingness of Pharisees to repent like the tax collectors. These walls are everywhere in Luke's Gospel. They represent resistance to the gospel of Jesus. But, just as the walls of Jericho came a tumblin' down, these walls do too. One person at a time.

"Zacchaeus was a wee little man," as the popular children's song goes. Like many of the people we have met in Luke's Gospel, he is also rich and a tax collector. Even more, he is the *chief* tax collector. One wonders whether he chose this line of work to cope with his inferiority complex. Little guys can pack a wallop when they are teased. I'm guessing Zacchaeus isn't very popular in Jericho. The people seem to know that he is a notorious sinner.

He climbs a sycamore tree to get a sight line on Jesus. Don't miss the irony. Zacchaeus, the powerful government tax collector, is lifted up in a sycamore tree to see the powerless one who is going to Jerusalem to be lifted up on a cross. And Jesus stops and asks to have dinner with him.

Similar to the complaint in Luke 15:1–2, the people gripe that he is, yet again, eating with sinners. This is one of the characteristic ways the kingdom of God comes—as hospitality toward and fellowship with the excluded. The meals Jesus shares with sinners, over and over again, foreshadow the Lord's Supper with his disciples, which becomes the sacrament of the presence of the Lord in the church.

In some encounters like this, Jesus defends the sinner about whom others are griping. Here, Jesus says nothing in defense of Zacchaeus. He is probably as bad as the people think he is. But all that is about to change. Just like the blind man outside the gate of Jericho a few verses earlier, this man can see. His response to the welcome of Jesus is repentance. He does half of what the rich ruler in chapter 18 could not do. He sells half his possessions and gives to the poor. He goes even further by offering the kind of justice the widow of chapter 18 sought but could not get. He gives back four times the amount he has defrauded from people—like poor widows.

Jesus announces a new identity for Zacchaeus. He is now a son of Abraham. No doubt he has never been called that before. Recall the lines of Abraham in the parable of Luke 16:19–31. This man has heard what the brothers of the man tormented in hell could not hear. He is being compassionate to the poor and doing right by his fellow man. Therefore, Jesus announces that salvation has come to Zacchaeus's house.

GOING DEEPER

Salvation is a wonderful word that is often given a very narrow meaning. In all its richness here, salvation means forgiveness for sin, restoration to God, inclusion in the community, and welcome at the synagogue. Zacchaeus is healed spiritually, relationally, and economically. His salvation is good news for everybody in town, not just for himself.

The Gospel of Luke is full of good things that happened at tables. Go looking for them. What does this pattern say about the practice of eating together?

CONSIDER THIS

1. As we reflect on the image of the wall of Jericho, what modern walls of resistance in our culture are erected to the gospel?

2. Who is Zacchaeus in your community?

3. Who is the blind man outside the walls?

4. In this story, repentance is tangible: money to the poor, restitution for cheating. How are these tangible results still part of forgiveness today?

ONE TOUGH KING

SCRIPTURE

Luke 19:11–27

THE BIG IDEA

The kingdom is coming in fullness. Jesus ushers in the kingdom and his disciples are the new Israel. We will account for our stewardship of the message entrusted to us.

CORE TEACHING

With the healing of a blind man and the repentance of Zacchaeus, it was not a far stretch to believe that the kingdom was close at hand. It's not every day you see things like this. Jesus tells a parable about waiting faithfully for the arrival of the kingdom.

In this parable, we are introduced to a king who is going on a journey to get royal power for himself. His servants cannot imagine living under his power because his kingdom is diametrically opposed to the way they have lived. It is a new, intrusive power that is coming. While they await the arrival of this kingdom, which is not here yet but is on the way, they are to do the master's work and tend to his interests.

In the parable, the third servant entrusted with money is thought by some scholars to be a reference to Israel. God gave Israel the Law and expected them to be a light to the nations. Israel, however, has failed to invest what was given and is now under judgment. What was given first to Israel is about to be given to others.

But scholars don't all agree on the implications of this particular parable, and it is not a far stretch to think that it is also about the disciples who have been traveling with Jesus, who have been blind to the understanding that the kingdom must come through suffering, and who are still expecting the kingdom's painless arrival. The disciples are called to be faithful stewards. Servants are expected to produce results from what they have been given.

The servants in the parable have earned their master's trust at three different levels. No doubt, their prior performance has caused the master to entrust to them amounts in keeping with that performance. To the top performer he entrusts the most, to the lowest the least.

The master's confidence in the first two servants proves justified. They are congratulated and given more responsibility. The third servant is an utter failure because he did not even try. His own response condemns him. He knows what his master wants—return on the investment. He does not open an interest-bearing account. He does not lend it out for interest. He does nothing in keeping with who he knows his master to be or what his master wants. By taking no action, he assures himself of the master's displeasure.

The parable calls us to faithful action on behalf of the coming King, even as we watch for his return. The reason the master is furious with the third slave is that, for a businessman, the whole point of money is that it be used, spent, and circulated to make more money. Money hoarded might as well be money thrown away. Our lives are to be expended in God's service, becoming the source of further blessing for others.

GOING DEEPER

This is another of Luke's odd parables. It takes parts of two different parables that we find in Matthew's Gospel and makes a little different point than either of those. The king is not quite Jesus, yet *is* Jesus. Luke gets us a bit off kilter to make us wrestle with truth. Jesus is coming with a new royal power, and many servants do not want to welcome him. Yet we are called to embrace the coming kingdom and to be about its business until the King comes. This parable can apply to the first *or* second coming of God. Herod and others resisted the first arrival.

Lest this begin to sound like merit-based salvation, it is important to note that good works (return on investments) are not what get us eternal life. We have already been given eternal life as the gracious entrustment of the Father. This parable is about is how life is meant to be lived—not in protection mode but in an aggressive partnership with God in the middle of the world. Burying what we have been given suggests that we neither know the Giver nor appreciate the gift. Saying yes to God comes with all kind of strings attached.

Lessons abound for disciples:

- We are always the *recipient* of all that we have but never the owner. It all goes back in the box at the end. God is the owner; we are stewards.

- We are not accountable for what we have not been given.
- God expects results from God's investment in us. We will answer for our lives.
- While we may be called to take risks, the only certain way to fail is not to even try. The person who loses their life for God's sake will find it.
- The more we succeed in using what we have been given, the more we will have entrusted to us.
- We can please God by our effective work if it is in keeping with God's interests in the world. Our responsible initiative pleases God.

CONSIDER THIS

1. How is God like the king in the parable?

2. How is God different from the king in the parable?

3. What has been entrusted to us by God?

4. What does God expect at his coming?

AND SO IT BEGINS

SCRIPTURE

Luke 19:28–44

THE BIG IDEA

This text moves us from the Jerusalem journey to the events of Holy Week. Three times Luke has told us the destination of the journey. Now we arrive, and the final confrontation begins. The entry into Jerusalem and the prayer on its behalf introduce Jesus's teaching in the temple. Most of chapters 20 and 21 occur in the temple. We experience the distance between the exuberant disciples and the plotting religious leaders. One of these groups will go home disappointed.

CORE TEACHING

We are coming to a bookend moment in the Gospel of Luke. Go back to Luke 1 and read the songs of Mary and Zechariah. These are the hopes of the common people: a ruler who shows mercy, scatters the proud, brings down the powerful, topples thrones, feeds the hungry, sends the rich away empty, rescues us from our enemies, gives light to those who sit in darkness, and guides our feet into the path of peace.

For nineteen chapters, Jesus has been doing all of these things. He has gathered into his hopeful entourage common fishermen, tax collectors, blind folk, lepers, women, Samaritans, gentiles, demoniacs, cripples, and prostitutes. He has told parables about a king like no other, ruling a kingdom like no other. The authority of his word has been experienced by centurions, the sick, and the dead. People believe. They have seen and heard enough to believe. Apparently the seed has fallen on good soil, and they have ears to hear what others cannot.

Jerusalem is no stranger to parades. Many have marched through her gates and down her streets. Kings, religious leaders, revolutionaries, and messianic figures. Each entrance is a parable of sorts, noting the kind of kingdom that ruler brings. Jesus's entrance on a donkey speaks humility in keeping with the prophecy of Zechariah 9. He is welcomed like God's kings should be, according to 2 Kings 9:13. The people spread their cloaks on the road and wave palm branches. Lest there be any who have not heard the news of Jesus, he is heralded as "the king who comes in the name of the Lord" (Luke 19:38).

Shall we join the parade? It looks like a victory march— but I detect the smell of death. Jesus has warned us as much. People are not lining the streets to join a procession to help the poor, to touch lepers, or to redeem tax collectors. Who wants to sign up to sell what you have and give it to the poor? Who is interested in scouring the hills for lost sheep? Who wants their overstuffed laughter turned to mourning? Who wants to sign up for loving their enemies? Who wants to go to pagan graveyards and bust demons? Who dares go face to face with people who have the power to crucify you? Just how big is this parade going to be?

The moviemakers tend to make it pretty big, but I don't know. It may have been smaller than we imagine. I'm guessing it isn't the biggest parade Jerusalem has ever seen because it doesn't have the kind of money, power, or advertising behind it that the Macy's Thanksgiving Day Parade has. When Herod throws a parade, he has backing. Jesus has little in the form of political, economic, or religious clout. In fact, he has no clout outside of the adoration of those whose lives have been forever changed by his words and deeds. But that's enough to make some noise. The Pharisees show up to check out the noise and ask the disciples to keep the racket down. Jesus responds on behalf of his followers, "If they keep quiet, the stones will cry out" (v. 40). The same Jesus who once refused to turn stones into bread now knows that stones can be turned into decibels if God's presence is denied.

We Christians want our faith to be on public parade, but we don't want to be embarrassed by it. But embarrassing is what the Christian parade of Jesus's followers *is*. It is a gathering of the rejects of humanity. It is a club for failures and outcasts. It is an assembly of sinners. If we want the power, glitz, glamour, and chic of the world, we better go and find another parade.

GOING DEEPER

As Jesus approaches the city, he cries. I've never seen anyone cry at their own parade. I believe Luke opens the heart of Jesus to us in this story. Jerusalem cannot understand that peace is coming to them on the back of a donkey—through the one who heals our disease, forgives our sin, makes us neighbors, delivers justice, shows mercy. Here he comes, riding on the back of a donkey. And in this moment he knows that we will reject him in favor of other kings. These kings will build armies, make war, tax everyone, sit on powerful thrones, enjoy privileges, ignore the needy, cater to the wealthy, and erect monuments to themselves. And as we bow to these kings, we will pay an awful price. It's enough to make Jesus weep.

CONSIDER THIS

1. In what ways is a parade a sign in the Gospel of Luke? What other parades or public gatherings are recorded in Luke?

2. How is the journey of Jesus to Jerusalem a staging of the people in the parade?

3. Of all the characters in Luke's Gospel, whom do you see making the most noise at the parade?

4. Do you believe God still weeps?

A TEMPEST IN THE TEMPLE

SCRIPTURE

Luke 19:45–21:38

THE BIG IDEA

In these two chapters, we hear the debates, teaching, and testing that occur in the temple during the week leading up to Jesus's crucifixion. The primary question revolves around the authority of Jesus, which is not a new idea in Luke's Gospel.

CORE TEACHING

Luke 19:45–48. The cleansing of the temple is a direct challenge to the authority of the religious leaders. The religious leaders have not felt unduly invaded by the ministry of Jesus in the highways and villages, but now the contest has come to their home court. The temple is their center of operation. And Jesus claims it for his Father as a house of prayer. We have been reminded of prayer by a widow

(18:1–8), a tax collector (18:9–14), and a blind man (18:35–43). Prayer invites a new kingdom. The commerce of the kingdom is God's will done, daily bread for all, forgiveness, and deliverance from the enemy. It is not profit from selling sacrificial animals. We are surprised that Luke does not use Mark's full phrase, "My house will be called a house of prayer for all nations" (11:17). This wording is certainly in keeping with the plot of Luke.

Luke 20:1–8. The religious leaders question the authority of Jesus on several fronts: his teaching, his claims regarding the kingdom, his familiarity with the Father, his words about Abraham, his parade entourage, his unsettling table-turnover in the temple. By what authority does he do these things? In our churches, authority is a big issue. We wrestle over the authority of the Scriptures. Different denominations posture themselves as authoritative voices on issues of faith. We preach and teach with authority. We declare people married on the basis of authority. We lay hands on people and ordain them by the authority of God. Without authority, we have little basis to do what we do. It is not a bad thing to question authority, especially when one comes among us claiming to speak and act in the name of God. They ask Jesus who gave him authority. He answers their question with a question about John the Baptist that places them on the horns of a dilemma, allowing him to escape their trap.

Luke 20:9–19. The parable of the vineyard owner and the rebellious tenants is easily understood in the temple. The vineyard is the people of God, God's choice planting. The owner and planter of the vineyard is the God of Abraham, Isaac, and Jacob. It is common knowledge that God sent prophets to tend the vine and that they were beaten, insulted, and sent away empty-handed by the rebellious tenants (see Isaiah 5). So the owner decided to send his son, believing the tenants would respect the son and give him the fruit of the vineyard. Instead, they killed the son in a hostile takeover. With the heir out of the way, they thought they could rule the vineyard. So the vineyard owner did what the religious leaders affirmed he should do: he went and destroyed the rebellious tenants and gave the vineyard to those who could be trusted. End of parable. Everyone agreed with the action of the owner of the vineyard—until Jesus identified *himself* as the Son who had been rejected.

Changing metaphors from farming to building, Jesus declares himself to be the cornerstone upon which everything rests. The religious leaders have rejected the cornerstone, and now that same stone falls on them, breaking them to pieces. They have rejected the son of the vineyard owner, the cornerstone of the temple of God, the Messiah from God. Caught in the trap of a parable, they want to kill Jesus—but they fear the people. I think the listening crowds knew exactly what Jesus was talking about.

Luke 20:20–26. The religious leaders have been soundly out-parabled in the previous verses, and now they find other sly conspirators to do their dirty work. If they can't get Jesus in trouble with religion, maybe they can get him crossways with the occupying Romans. The trap fails, of course, but it does net us the oft-quoted, "give back to Caesar what is Caesar's, and to God what is God's" (v. 25). Some have viewed this as Jesus's support for separation of church and state, but it's more like answering the question, "What does God *not* own?" When it comes to the kingdom, there is no higher power. Had Jesus said it that way, he would have been immediate toast. But he evades the testing of his authority again and lives to debate another group.

Luke 20:27–47. Meet the Sadducees. They have not appeared frequently in Luke's Gospel until now. They have specific beliefs about resurrection (specifically, that resurrection doesn't exist), and they, like all who have come before them, are trying to trap Jesus with a hypothetical scenario. A man marries a woman, and the man dies. The woman then marries his brother, and he dies. She marries the next brother, and he dies. You get the drift. Seven brothers die. And the question is whose wife will she be in the resurrection? (I'd have asked a different question: What was she putting in the soup?!) Jesus goes on to speak of the resurrection as a realm where marriage does not occur. I do not believe Jesus's assertion negates the covenant of Christian marriage on earth. It simply states that the necessary arrangements of this age will no longer be required in the eternal kingdom. Jesus goes on to affirm through illustrations of Moses and David that God is the God of the living, even though they have died. In God, all the people of God are alive.

Luke 21:1–4. We meet some of Luke's old friends here in the temple: rich people and a widow. They seem to be staple characters in this Gospel. We have just been told in Luke 20:47 that the scribes devour widows' houses. If this is true, she must not have much left in the bank account. Yet here she is, dropping two small copper coins in the temple treasury. Jesus does not oppose temple offerings, but he does recognize a big gift when he sees it. It is always attached to the size of sacrifice. She is doing what the rich ruler of Luke 18:18 could not bring himself to do—giving all that she has.

GOING DEEPER

Luke 21:5–24. Jesus paints a bleak future for Jerusalem—not one stone left on top of another, war, earthquake, famine, disease, persecution for being a follower of Jesus, betrayal by family members, fleeing from an approaching enemy, the woes of pregnant women, death by sword, and captivity. It sounds a lot like the world we live in today, doesn't it?

Historically, this came to be an accurate description of the fall of Jerusalem within a generation of Jesus's temple visit. But buried within the warning are also words of assurance. We will be given wise words that our opponents will not be able to withstand or contradict. (This is just what we saw Jesus do in response to the attempts of religious leaders to trap him.) And, by our endurance, our souls will be gained. Or, in more current vernacular, we will be true to our identity as the followers of the persecuted, crucified, resurrected Son of God.

CONSIDER THIS

1. In what ways is Jesus a great debater?

2. Why is authority the main issue? What is at stake here?

3. Which of the challenges of chapter 20 is closest to where you live your life?

4. How will you fare under religious persecution?

READY OR NOT

SCRIPTURE

Luke 21:25–38

THE BIG IDEA

The oddity of the return of the Lord in a postmodern age causes many of us to skip this text. It feels strange. But maybe a world desperately needing redemption will not be saved by common intervention. We require a salvation that comes from beyond us and does what centuries of Christian presence has not been able to do: make the world right.

CORE TEACHING

"Ready or not, here I come!"

And with those words, the hunter of the hunted comes to find every cringing, hiding player of the game. *Ready or not, here I come.* The one who is It will wait no longer.

Luke is interested in something he calls "the coming of the Son of Man." He uses eschatological code language for the move of God to set the world straight. God really intends to make things right. We tend to call this the second coming. It may seem strange that these texts are often in the Common Lectionary as Advent texts. But, as much as the story of Mary and Joseph is about God's coming, so is Luke 21. "Ready or not," says Luke, "here comes Jesus."

Okay. When? When is the Son of Man coming? We'll put it on our schedule.

The thing is, no one knows. Not the angels in heaven. Not the authors of *Left Behind.* Not the soothsayers with the end-time charts. Not even the Son of Man himself. No one knows—which is, frankly, unsettling. We academic types are all about *knowing*—and if we don't know, we'll find out. I mean, we've got libraries, labs, laptops. Surely the coming of the Son of Man can be googled! Do you know why not knowing is unsettling to us? If we don't know, we don't have control. If we don't know, we're not in charge.

The coming of the Lord will reveal us for who we really are. While on the surface we may look the same, the coming of the Son of Man separates us into the ready and the not ready. So what are we to do with this?

I find myself thinking about college students. They grew up in a world with a lot of harsh realities and tragedies: mass shootings like Sandy Hook, the Charleston church, and the Orlando nightclub; natural and devastating disasters like earthquakes, tornadoes, wildfires, and hurricanes all over the world; renewed outbreaks of viruses and illnesses we thought we were close to eradicating, and on and on. They are aware that any one of these incidents could happen to them. They are not desensitized to tragedy, but they're not surprised by it either. Their generation seems to bear the burden of knowing the unthinkable will happen. Towers, cities, and the sense of security they have will falter and topple at times. They tend to shield themselves from becoming invested in the issues of the day. As a generation, they've learned to compartmentalize and make such incidents impersonal because they know another tragedy lurks around the next corner.

It strikes me that this is how many feel about the coming of the Son of Man. I think preachers of Luke are partly responsible for it. He writes about the coming of the Son of Man like a catastrophe, a tragedy, a tsunami, a thief, a monstrous terror—which is how apocalyptic language tended to work in biblical days.

But what if it takes some unsettling of the way things are to set the world right? What if we need more than rearranging, patching, or a new coat of paint? What if everything dead needs to be revealed as dead so that everything God loves can be resurrected, made new, and given life?

If that's what it takes, then we're in for a grand and glorious unsettling. The first Advent was unsettling. He came into the world threatening Herod's government, suggesting peace rather than war, and talking about the last being first and the first being last; about the meek inheriting the earth; about rulers serving; about prostitutes getting into the kingdom ahead of the holiness crowd; about laying down your life.

"Ready or not, here I come."

GOING DEEPER

I tried to remember the last time I walked around thinking, *The Son of Man may come today.* I couldn't remember. Anybody wake up this morning thinking about the return of Jesus? How do you live in readiness for a moment you can't predict or know? And why be alert to what you can't stop or escape?

I have a hard time concentrating on this present moment. It's a slippery thing. Got it! Oops—it's gone. There comes one—no, that's future—missed it, past. My *now* is pretty full of figuring out the past and worrying about the future. And if I could live in awareness of the coming of the Son of Man, would I really want to be locked in, moment by moment, on an unknown date, an unstoppable flood, an unveiling judgment?

In a world of religious speculation, the coming of God is meant to be a message of hope and redemption rather than a scare tactic to get people to straighten up and fly right. Is there any good news in these texts?

CONSIDER THIS

1. What emotion rises in you when you contemplate the return of Jesus?

2. Why have speculative movies and novels informed our second-coming theology more than the Bible has?

3. Imagine the coming of the Lord today. How would the world be different?

MORE LESSONS AROUND A TABLE

SCRIPTURE

Luke 22:1–38

THE BIG IDEA

The Passover gathering is the last time we see Jesus alone with his disciples in a teaching mode. If last words carry deep meaning, the church would do well to heed these.

CORE TEACHING

Luke 22:1–6. The setting of the next six sections of the Gospel is the Feast of Passover. It calls to mind the slaves of Egypt gathering around their tables for one final meal before their journey to the promised land began. During the dark night of deliverance, God dealt with the powers that had enslaved his people. Numerous warnings by way of plagues had not been enough to gain their freedom. It would take blood—the blood of every firstborn son of Egypt. Every year after that, the Jews gathered at the Feast of Unleavened Bread to remember Passover, the night the death angel passed over them and required life in exchange for freedom. These texts are troublesome. The idea of God killing firstborn sons is hard, be it Isaac son of Abraham, the infant boys of Egypt, or his only begotten Son.

Luke 22:7–38. Passover arrives. Luke mentions the sacrificial lamb, and we see the shadow of the cross hanging over Jesus. Preparations are made as a house is provided much the same way the donkey for the parade entry was provided—by a person they encounter. Once again, we find hospitality from a stranger who opens his house to Jesus and the disciples for a Passover meal. They gather in a large, upper room. As the meal begins, Jesus again speaks of the suffering that is ahead. But this time he announces that it will be the final meal he shares with them until the kingdom is fulfilled. Make no mistake that the breaking of bread in Luke 24 is connected to this promise at this table. Only then, the post-resurrection meal will share in the body and blood of the Lord of freedom. The blood of the sacrificial Passover lamb will be the blood of the risen Jesus.

The formula that we saw earlier is here. Jesus takes the bread, blesses it, breaks it, and gives it to his disciples. What Jesus does with bread was done to him. He was taken/chosen as the Son of God at birth and baptism, blessed of the Father as the beloved Son, broken by rejection and crucifixion, and given away to the disciples through the gift of the Spirit. And now he teaches the disciples to gather at the table and live out the pattern. We are the people of God, laid claim to at our baptism. We are the broken people of God, sharing in the sufferings of Jesus for the redemption of the world. And we are the given people of God, sent out into the world in the name of Jesus to preach, heal, and declare the arrival of the kingdom.

From here, the narrative begins to focus on different disciples at the table. One is identified as the betrayer. But which one? Is it the one who sells Jesus to the highest bidders and plots with them to find a quiet alley to jump him? Or is it disciples who argue about which of them is the greatest in the room? Jesus quickly dissolves the argument by saying that greatness equals service in his kingdom. They will soon learn the hard way that greatness has lots of suffering mixed in. Or is the betrayer the one Satan sifts like wheat, the one who will deny knowing Jesus three times before the cock crows the morning alarm? He thinks he is ready to fight in allegiance—and maybe he is because Jesus says the two swords they have might come in handy. There are lots of ways to betray Jesus.

GOING DEEPER

This text reintroduces a character we have seen little of since Luke 4:1. The devil is back. He is doing the same thing here that he did in chapter 4: seeking to divert Jesus from his mission. Many believe that Judas wanted Jesus to make a forceful declaration that his messianic intentions were nationalistic—that he had come to run the Romans out of town. I don't know. We aren't given much more than Satan entering Judas, planting the seeds of betrayal in his heart. Either way, the deal is struck. A price is set. And the plan is put in place to arrest Jesus when there isn't a crowd around to stop them.

We should not make this a spook text, where the devil becomes the dark power sneaking around and taking over unsuspecting people and making them do what they don't want to do. Instead, this text tells us that, behind every dark deed we have conspired to do, we are participating in a larger darkness that exists only to steal, kill, and destroy. Evil is bigger than our individual deeds. It is corporate in nature but works its ways through humans.

The spine of the narrative is the Passover Feast and the conversations that happen around the table before, during, and after. These things are still going on at the table of God. Satan is at work. But so is Jesus, teaching us what greatness is and how we can pattern our lives after his.

CONSIDER THIS

1. Have you ever experienced Satan putting something into your heart? What was it like?

2. When you share Holy Communion/Eucharist, what do you experience?

3. Why did this sacramental act become the defining ritual of the Christian church rather than something like the foot washing or laying hands on people?

4. Given Jesus's definition of greatness, who is the greatest person you know today?

IN THE GARDEN

SCRIPTURE

Luke 22:39–62

THE BIG IDEA

Jesus willingly accepts the cross, step by step. This is the beginning of his ending. And even here, he teaches us the way of the kingdom even as he reveals the ways of darkness.

CORE TEACHING

The final moment of prayer comes as Jesus asks the Father for another way. "If you are willing, take this cup from me; yet not my will, but yours be done" (v. 42). We hear echoes from earlier in the Gospel. In the wilderness of temptation, Satan offered Jesus a much easier way to rule the kingdoms of the world. Jesus turned him down cold. In the prayer of Luke 11, he told his disciples to pray, "thy kingdom come, thy will be done on earth." The time has come for Jesus to live out the prayer.

Three separate times in the Gospel Jesus announced to the disciples that he was going to Jerusalem to be arrested, tortured, and crucified. The garden of Gethsemane is not a surprise to Jesus. The Father has not sprung a new mission on Jesus at the last minute. Jesus has understood his role as the Suffering Servant of Israel, the sacrificial Lamb of the Passover, the crucified Messiah.

He tries to warn his disciples to pray themselves strong. Is that even possible? All we are capable of when Judas arrives with the armed guards is whacking off an ear. We can't stop what the powers of darkness do in gardens of grief and betrayal. We may hack away at the darkness, but it still wins. It waits for the opportune moment, and when we are found sleeping instead of praying, fighting instead of obeying, it does its dirty work.

In a miracle of grace, Jesus heals the severed ear of one of his accusers, the slave of the high priest. Here's another nameless peon in Luke's Gospel who gets a taste of the kingdom when it is least deserved. I wonder how he would feel about the night ahead.

Peter is in for a long night himself. He follows the arrest party at a distance and hangs around the edges of the action. I like this about Peter. He cannot walk away. We don't know where the rest of them are. This is the first time they have been without Jesus in a long time. The way Luke tells the story, they have been there every step of the way since the calling of the disciples in chapter 5.

Peter lingers behind. I find it interesting that here he is called Peter. At the supper a few verses earlier, Jesus called him Simon. The rock turns to gravel as people begin to recognize him. Three times, just like the prophet Jesus

said, Peter denies knowing Jesus or being one of the followers. He finally blurts out, "Man, I don't know what you're
talking about!" (v. 60). One of the Gospels suggests that he
curses. The cock crows. Peter weeps bitterly.

When it costs to follow Jesus, there are always conve-
nient ways out. But they always end in bitter tears of regret.

GOING DEEPER

Many congregations visit this text on the evening of
Maundy Thursday. It is often read in conjunction with the
Last Supper text. The only way for us to prepare for what is
ahead is to confess our place in the story. We too have fallen
asleep. We are not up to the challenge of facing the darkness on our own. Something must happen on our behalf if
we are to face the dark night of the soul when evil comes
looking to do us in. But Jesus has gone to the garden in our
place and has prayed for us there. And now he will make
his way to the cross and die in our place.

CONSIDER THIS

1. What do you think Jesus and the Father talked about
   that night in the garden?

2. When have you had a Gethsemane in your life?

3. Why does Luke include the parts about the sword
   (verses 36–38 and 49–51)?

4. When Jesus says to the Father, "yet not my will, but
   yours be done," is this resignation to fate or participation
   in mission?

JESUS THE PROPHET

SCRIPTURE

Luke 22:63–65

THE BIG IDEA

Throughout his Gospel, Luke has identified Jesus as a prophet. In this text, the soldiers have blindfolded Jesus and are mocking and beating him, demanding that he prophesy which one of them is hitting him. This text is a companion to several others that identify Jesus as a prophet.

CORE TEACHING

Prophecy in Luke is a major theme. The Old Testament prophets were filled with the Spirit of God to speak on behalf of God. More than foretelling the future, the prophet was engaged in foretelling the coming kingdom. John the Baptist was considered to be the last in the line of prophets, but Jesus is also distinctly identified as a prophet.

Biblical theology often explains the ministry of Jesus as a fulfillment of the three primary roles of the Old Testament: prophet, priest, and king. All are found in Luke, but the dominant role is that of the prophet. He comes filled with the Spirit, as the mouthpiece of God, mighty in word and deed, threatening the powers of darkness, opposed by the devil, and critical of religious leaders. In Luke 4, three times we are told that Jesus is filled with the Spirit. His hometown rejects him and the statement is made, "A prophet has no honor in his hometown."

In Luke 7, Jesus enters the town of Nain and interrupts a funeral procession. A widow has lost her adult son, her sole means of support. Jesus raises him to life, and the people declare, "A great prophet has appeared among us" (v. 16). A little later in chapter 7, a sinful woman is anointing Jesus's feet, and the host Pharisee, Simon, says, "If this man were a prophet, he would know who is touching him and what kind of woman she is—that she is a sinner" (v. 39). Tucked in between these two prophet stories is the query of John the Baptist sending followers to ask if Jesus is the one, the Messiah. The prophet is asking the prophet of his identity. Jesus answers him, "The blind receive sight, the lame walk, those who have leprosy are cleansed, the deaf hear, the dead are raised, and the good news is proclaimed to the poor" (v. 22).

In Luke 13, the storm of rejection darkens, and Jesus is warned that Herod wants to kill him. He is encouraged to flee Jerusalem. Jesus replies, "It is impossible for a prophet to be killed outside of Jerusalem. Jerusalem, Jerusalem, the city that kills the prophets and stones those who are sent to it!" (vv. 33–34, NRSV). Jesus views the opposition to him in the same vein as the opposition to the prophets of old.

Jesus is eventually arrested and accused of being a false prophet for blaspheming and for speaking of the destruction of the temple. He is blindfolded, and soldiers mock and beat him, demanding that he prophesy which one of them is hitting him.

In Luke 24, the two traveling in sadness on the Emmaus Road identify Jesus (who has just been crucified in Jerusalem) as "Jesus of Nazareth, who was a prophet mighty in deed and word before God and all the people" (v. 19, NRSV). They express their shattered hope that he might have been the Messiah. Then the unrecognized Jesus begins with Moses and the prophets and explains how the Messiah must suffer. Their hearts are warmed and, later, their eyes opened to see the risen Jesus.

As the risen Messiah, he now becomes the bearer of the Spirit, the one who breathes on them and fills them with the same Spirit that empowered him. The resurrection is the vindication of Jesus.

GOING DEEPER

While Luke's Gospel is about the salvation of the gentiles, outsiders, and excluded ones, it is also deeply rooted in the history of the people of God. The role of the prophet is the residence of hope in the Old Testament. It is fitting that Jesus fulfills the hope of humankind by being the prophet of God, mighty in word and deed.

Prophets painted pictures of a preferred future. More than being predictors, they were imaginative storytellers of what God's desired future looks like. Read Isaiah 9:1–9, 11:1–9, and 40:1–11.

CONSIDER THIS

1. How does Jesus embody the role of the prophet in the book of Luke?

2. Where in the church today do you see people playing the role of the prophet?

3. Why is the Spirit necessary for the mission of God?

4. What is it like to be filled with the Holy Spirit?

JESUS FACES THE RULING POWER

SCRIPTURE

Luke 22:66–23:25

THE BIG IDEA

In four brief scenes we are walked through the way power deals with the sacrificial Lamb. Each authority figure questions him from a unique position of power but ultimately engages in jurisdictional squabbles that end in passing the buck to the next guy.

CORE TEACHING

Luke 22:66–71. The hastily convened council of religious leaders gathers to seal the deal. Their minds are made up. They have heard his teaching, and they know what people think. Jesus, recognizing that his time has come, does not debate with them as he did earlier in the temple.

He is careful not to put a bullet in their gun. "Are you the Messiah?" they ask him.

"You wouldn't believe me if I told you. But from now on, you will find me seated at the right hand of the power of God."

Which prompts another question from them: "So you are saying that you are the Son of God?"

Again, a careful answer. "You say that I am."

He gives them just enough rope to hang him.

Luke 23:1–5. But they need a henchman to do their deadly work, so they drag Jesus before Pilate. He has no interest in their religious debates and does not wish to be on the wrong end of the demise of a popular figure. They throw in some political innuendoes—forbids us to pay taxes to the emperor (not exactly what he said but close enough); perverts the nation (religious speak for "lawbreaker"); calls himself a king, a messiah. Pilate declares insufficient evidence and bids them go home.

In an aside, they mention that Jesus has been stirring up trouble in Galilee. Now Pilate knows what to do. Pass the buck.

Luke 23:6–12. He sends him to the ruling power over Galilee, who just happens to be in town that very day. Herod has heard about Jesus, no doubt in conjunction with the ordeal surrounding John the Baptist. People in Galilee have been reporting miracles, and Herod is in a mood to see one. Jesus refuses to do any magic tricks but stands silently as they all mock him, costume him with a royal robe, and have a good time making fun of him. Gift-wrapped like a king, Herod sends him back to Pilate.

The power barons of Jerusalem are playing ping-pong with the Son of Man. And religious leaders are enjoying the show. Pilate and Herod become good friends that day.

Both names will be remembered forever. One even garners a mention in the Apostles' Creed. Both are kings who long have been food for worms while the one they taunt will sit as their judge on resurrection morning.

Luke 23:13–25. The court of appeal spreads to a public porch. Pilate announces that there is insufficient evidence to warrant death. With his pass-the-buck option exhausted, he decides to have Jesus flogged and released. Suddenly the crowd is energized, and they request Barabbas over Jesus. Luke, ever the historian, does a little backtracking in the text to inform us about Barabbas. But we have to go next door to the other Gospels to get the full story of the ritual of releasing a prisoner.

Pilate protests the popular request, but the crowd grows more vocal. Not only do they want Barabbas released, they also want Jesus crucified. So the insurrectionist-murderer is set free, and the Prince of Peace is dragged away to be killed. If you ask me, they released the less dangerous man—because the one they killed was about to turn history upside down. His insurrection would topple every dark power and bring justice to every murderer. It would usurp every throne and bring every knee to the earth in confession. It would establish him as King of kings and Lord of lords. If they wanted to keep their dark world, they killed the wrong man.

GOING DEEPER

Some say that Jesus's statement, "You say that **I am**," is a designation of divinity. Jesus is stating that he is the Son of God. The Gospel of John uses this formula to identify Jesus as God. John gives us Jesus declaring, "I am the light of the world," "I am the good shepherd," "I am the true vine," and more. Spend some time looking for other "I am" sayings of Jesus in the Gospel of John.

The interesting thing about the exchange in Luke 22:66–71 is the use of power language by Jesus, the only powerless one in the room. He speaks of ascending to the throne and sitting at the right hand of the power of God. And he uses the "I am" language that comes from the Old Testament name for God, *Yahweh*. They believe they are putting an end to Jesus. Jesus knows that a new kingdom is beginning. We can live in either reality; that is our choice as recipients of free will. But only one reality ends in resurrection.

CONSIDER THIS

1. What do you think is running through the mind of Jesus during this series of inquiries and judgments?

2. What other times in the history of Christianity have religious leaders been dead wrong about judgments placed on servants of God?

3. When have you failed to see the activity of God and misjudged someone who was actually trying to save you?

4. Why did the crowd choose Barabbas?

THE DAY THE SUN REFUSED TO SHINE

SCRIPTURE

Luke 23:26–56

THE BIG IDEA

The crucifixion story of Luke draws on Old Testament references as well as elements of the gospel. It unfolds in five scenes.

CORE TEACHING

Luke 23:26–31. We meet another stranger, Simon of Cyrene. This parade of suffering is much different from the earlier parade. This one has foreigners and wailing women. They join in a lament that is customary in death parades. They beat their chests and wail loud cries of anguish. Jesus has already lamented the fate of Jerusalem. Now he tells them to join in his weeping for the city because the dark days ahead will be even worse than this dark day.

Luke 23:32–38. The mocking continues as religious leaders and soldiers scoff and taunt the crucified one. Even as they do, Jesus offers forgiveness. His kingship is a joke to them. His royal robe is now the prize of a roll of the dice. In moments of great humiliation, it takes a God like Jesus to pray forgiveness. When we are at our worst, God is still God. Our evil does not blot out his mercy.

Luke 23:39–43. One of the criminals gets in on the teasing. Maybe he thought he could curry favor with his executioners. Or maybe he was revealing the dark heart that put him there. But the other criminal defends Jesus and expresses a form of faith. He reminds us of the parade of people who happened upon Jesus in their deepest need and came away with sight, hearing, life, bread, or pardon. This man, as a result of his declaration, is promised fellowship with Jesus in paradise.

Luke 23:44–49. Jesus goes to his death entrusting himself to the Father. He commends his breath into the hands of God. *Breath* is the word for Spirit. What leaves Jesus in this moment will be returned to him by the Father, only now it will be enough for everyone to share. Soon a rushing, mighty wind-breath will fill the disciples, and they will experience, according to the book of Acts, pure hearts and divine power.

Luke 23:50–56. The ordeal ends with the body of Jesus being claimed by a good and righteous man named Joseph. Not every Jew in Luke's Gospel is like the bloodthirsty crowd. We've met Elizabeth and Zechariah, Mary and Joseph, Simeon and Anna, the twelve disciples, and many other good insiders along the way. The thing that makes this Joseph different is that he comes from a town that is waiting expectantly for the kingdom of God. He is an early hint of those who will soon wait in an upper room for the same kingdom, the same holy breath, the same Jesus. And they will not be disappointed. Joseph follows custom and buries Jesus appropriately, laying him to rest in a rock-hewn tomb.

And accompanying him are the women. These precious women have been there through the parade of lament, the merciless mockery, the taunting criminal, the prayer of forgiveness for the executioners, darkness, and death. They have seen it all. They go with Jesus to the bitter end, and they leave him in a tomb. Their following is over.

Or is it?

GOING DEEPER

The seven last words from the cross enable us to see what God is doing. In the Luke account, God-in-Christ is offering up lament for the world, forgiving his enemies, yielding himself to the mission of God, offering grace to a dying man, and dying. The cross also allows us to see what humans are capable of: mockery of the sacred, murder of hope, and robbery of life. We do all quite proficiently.

Luke tells us that the veil of the temple was torn in two. We veil that which is holy to respect its dignity and to protect it from usage that will cheapen it. The veil before the Holy of Holies was a way of saying to humans that boundaries are to be respected, just as God expected us to respect the boundary around the tree in the garden of Eden. Relationships of dignity call for respect. To enter behind the veil into the Holy of Holies without due devotion or commitment was deadly.

I think I may have misunderstood this text for a long time. At Jesus's death, the veil of the temple is rent, exposing the Holy of Holies. I always thought previously that in this moment the Spirit of God was loosed into the world. But what if this text is telling us that, by stripping Jesus naked on the cross, trampling on the dignity of our Creator, and treating him as an object of execution, we violated the dignity of our humanity? Holiness is unveiled by evil in the cross. God's holiness is stripped naked of the sacred veil. This is the epitome of evil. And then a miracle of grace occurs. We gaze upon pure, holy love.

CONSIDER THIS

1. Which character do you relate to most in the story of the crucifixion?

2. What does the rending of the veil of the temple mean?

3. Where are the twelve disciples? Why are the women still there, and why aren't the men?

4. What does the death of Jesus mean to you?

THE FIRST GLIMPSE
OF KINGDOM

SCRIPTURE

Luke 24:1–12

THE BIG IDEA

The confirmation of everything Jesus told them is right in front of their eyes. They begin to wrestle with believing what their eyes see and their ears hear. We are reminded of the parable of the sower. Will they have eyes to see and ears to hear the good news?

CORE TEACHING

The women, last seen at the cross and tomb, are back on the first day of the week. They have come with spices. It is reminiscent of how we often come to worship on the first day of the week—expecting to make things nice but not prepared to behold the resurrection. The stone is gone.

Someone else has been there. Two men in dazzling clothes appear. We have seen this before, on the Mount of Transfiguration. There is no hint that this is Moses and Elijah, but we don't know that it isn't either.

Whoever it is, the darkness of noon the day before has now been transformed into light. Resurrection light is hard to look at head on. They look at the ground in fear. All of this is a normal reaction to being in the presence of the divine.

And the messengers say the words that humanity has longed to hear. "Why do you look for the living among the dead? He is not here; he has risen!" (24:6). These words are the very hinge of history. If they are true, everything changes.

They remember what Jesus told them, and they rush away to tell the others, the eleven, the men. Their names are recorded by Luke. They are the first eyewitnesses of his majesty and glory. Lest women be considered unordainable, let's remember they were the first to be entrusted with the news of the resurrection. And the men hear the gospel first from women. Like many men I know, the disciples think it is pure fascination, an idle tale.

Peter has to see for himself. He can't take a woman's word for it. He runs to the tomb, stoops and looks in, and sees the linen clothes, exactly as the women have said. And, of all things, he goes home amazed.

Each Gospel has disciples doing different things: joining Jesus on the road to Galilee, going fishing, hiding in fear. But only here does Peter just go home, amazed. The next time we see him will be Acts 1. And, before we know it, he'll be preaching the resurrection of Jesus all over Jerusalem. But for now, he goes home. I wonder what he told his wife and mother-in-law.

GOING DEEPER

The incomprehensibility of the resurrection cannot be explained in a way that makes sense. N. T. Wright's *The Resurrection of the Son of God* is a wonderful gift to the church. Wright offers confidence that the resurrection narratives could not be contrived or made up. People would not have done what the women and disciples did in these accounts. Women would not have been written in as eyewitnesses just for fun. Disciples would not have gone home amazed. We'd have heroic stories and miracles galore, if it was made up. But what we have instead is human fear and amazement and pure, unfiltered reaction. That's all God expects from us still: that we experience the resurrection as real people.

CONSIDER THIS

1. Why do the disciples play such a small role in Luke's Gospel as compared with the other Gospels? Why do the women play a larger role for Luke?

2. Where else in the Bible do we find two men in dazzling white clothes?

3. Track the things Peter has experienced firsthand over the past few days.

4. When was the first time it dawned on you that Jesus of Nazareth is alive?

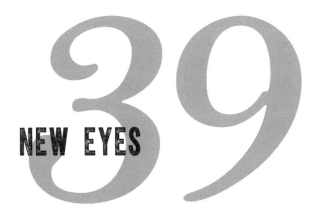

NEW EYES

SCRIPTURE

Luke 24:13–35

THE BIG IDEA

This is the primary resurrection story of Luke. It serves as a bridge to the book of Acts. Several themes of the Gospel are picked up, and the re-definition of Messiah and kingdom come full circle as hearts are warmed and eyes opened.

CORE TEACHING[1]

Are your eyes old? Does your mind decide in advance what it's going to see? Are you so conditioned by the same-old, same-old that your perspective is narrowed to the expected? I recognize that eyes flatten with age and vision can

1. Dan Boone, *Preaching the Story that Shapes Us* (Kansas City, MO: Beacon Hill Press of Kansas City, 2008), 207–12.

be a chronological thing. But old eyes can happen at any age, to anyone. Old eyes are a problem all over the world.

- In the Middle East, Palestinians look at Jews, and Jews look at Palestinians, and all either one of them sees is the enemy.
- In marriages, he looks at her, and she looks at him—and he's always like this, and she's always like that.
- In college dorms people get pegged a certain way, put in a box, and everyone sees them through the knothole of that box. Old eyes won't let them out.
- In politics, the Democrats see those fiscally tight, rich-courting Republicans, and the Republicans see those tax-and-spend, bleeding-heart liberals, and Washington is gridlocked.
- In the economic world, the rich see the poor, and the poor see the rich, and both have choice things to say about the other.
- In the church world, the Calvinists see holy-roller Wesleyans, and the Wesleyans see sin-every-day-in-word-thought-and-deed Calvinists.
- Even in the bathroom mirror, old eyes are a problem. Some see more than they ought, courtesy of a bloated ego; others see less than they ought, courtesy of low self-esteem.

I hear you pushing back at me already. You're saying: Past performance is a good indicator of future performance. Old dogs rarely learn new tricks. Leopards don't change their spots. Humans are set in their ways. The habits we form dig grooves in our brains, and where we've been, we'll go again because repeat performance is instinctive.

I know. I hear you. I say the same thing most of the time. This old world of ours is settling into its dying ways, doing the same deadly thing over and over. We see so much of it that our eyes come to expect it. We even see it coming before it ever gets here. I know what you say.

But there is a story in our Bible about old eyes and new eyes. Could I tell you that story?

It's based on Luke 24:13–35.

It's Sunday. The Sunday after crucifixion Friday. Last Sunday they had a gleam in their eyes. They were following Jesus and had come to expect divine surprises, like lepers healed, little girls getting up from death beds and asking for something to eat, prostitutes changing careers, sinners coming home for dinner, multitudes fed from sack lunches. Following Jesus had given them new eyes. They had come to expect to see the world in ways they had only dreamed of before.

And then came that fateful Friday—which confirmed that, if something seems too good to be true, it probably is. They got their old eyes back, courtesy of a cruel crucifixion that left no doubt as to who runs the world. The same old, deadly powers were still at it.

Why hope? It's a terrible thing to lose hope. I've lost it a few times in my life. Movies like *Roots* and *Hotel Rwanda* and *Schindler's List* depress me for days. To see what humans are capable of doing to their fellow humans just takes all the optimism for humanity right out of you.

The two on the road to Emmaus knew exactly how that felt. And they decided to go home. Jesus joined them on their journey. The text tells us very carefully that they were kept from recognizing him. We are not told how or why. Maybe they were blinded by grief. Maybe his hands and feet were hidden inside a baggy robe. Maybe the crucifixion had altered him beyond recognition. Maybe they were just looking down the whole time. I don't know. Do you?

I'm guessing these two were husband and wife. If you look at the conversation carefully, it looks to me like they kept interrupting each other, finishing each other's sentences. One would start and the other finish. Makes sense if you think about them inviting Jesus in at the end of the walk and setting the table and making up the guest room.

The conversation on the road is what intrigues me. They explained to Jesus what had happened in Jerusalem as if he had not gotten word of it. They talked about their dead hopes. Jesus just listened. He let them talk. And when he did start talking, he gave them a biblical review of all the law and prophets. The topic was suffering—which they wanted to avoid as much as possible. But the stranger believed that you could not tell the story of God without suffering being part of it.

Cleopas and companion knew the script. Messiah comes, Messiah is enthroned, Messiah reigns. That's how the story goes. The stranger offered a different plot line, though. Messiah comes, Messiah is rejected, Messiah is crucified, Messiah is dead and buried, Messiah is raised. They had never anticipated this plot line. They could not see God at work in what had happened in Jerusalem last Friday.

Maybe they were living the wrong script, taking their cues from a bad story. Could it be that God is most at work when everything seems to be falling apart? Can you see God at work in those places? Hard, isn't it?

They invited him to come in and stay with them. "It's too late to travel any farther. We have an empty room, and you can join us for supper." And when he broke the bread, their eyes were opened. Just as carefully as the text tells us they were kept from recognizing him, it now tells us that their eyes were opened. It does not say, "They opened their eyes;" rather, it says, "Their eyes *were* opened" (v. 31). The verbs here are important. These two were not acting; they were being acted upon. Forces beyond them were doing things to their eyes that they did not control.

This is a great place for me to come out of the phone booth with my SuperPreacher cape on. I could wow you with three points on how to open your eyes or tell you the four secrets of seeing what you never saw before or the five principles of spiritual insight.

But I can't. I don't know any more than you do how their eyes were opened. They just were. New eyes are a gift.

GOING DEEPER

Do you remember when the *Magic Eye* pictures came out? There were objects hidden inside the pictures. You had to look at the pictures a certain way to see the hidden forms and shapes. Marty and Ruth were passing through our town and stopped by to see us. They had purchased one of these books in Chicago. I had never seen these pictures before. They had a picture of a beach scene. They said if we looked in the water, we'd see two dolphins. We all looked. My wife saw them. My two teenage daughters saw them. My five-year-old saw them. I didn't see them.

They told me to squint. "Now hold the picture close to your face and pull it away slowly. Look *through* the picture." I tried everything and never saw any dolphins. I was almost ready to believe it was a trick until Danielle, our neighbor friend, stopped by unexpectedly. It took her about thirty seconds to see the dolphins.

That night everyone was upstairs sleeping, and I was still downstairs, squinting and looking cross-eyed at two invisible dolphins. I never did see them. I went to the mall and saw these pictures in every store window. People stood there saying, "Look, a pyramid. Look, Elvis. Look, a motorcycle." I saw nothing. I bought the book of pictures. What

NEW EYES

187

you were supposed to see was shaded in in the back of the book. I could tell you what was on every page, but I couldn't see it.

Then one day, when I was almost not looking, my eyes were opened.

New eyes are a gift. You may not see the risen Jesus, but he is walking with you right now, interpreting the script of your life. His story is different from any story you've ever heard before.

And when Jesus opens your eyes, enemies will look like neighbors. A spouse will look like the one you vowed to love, honor, and cherish. People at school will look different than their confining boxes. Politicians will look like people who can work together for a larger cause. The poor will look needy; the rich will look like they can help. Calvinists will look like brothers and sisters. Wesleyans will look like people with open arms. And the person in the bathroom mirror will look like—of all things—a beloved child of God.

CONSIDER THIS

1. Why did the two on the road not recognize Jesus?

2. Where else in Luke's Gospel do we find blind people or people who have eyes but do not see?

3. What is it about faith that uses the analogy of sight to describe the life of a disciple?

4. When was the last time your heart was warmed by the presence of the resurrected Christ?

HANDS AND FEET

SCRIPTURE

Luke 24:36–42

THE BIG IDEA

The incarnation continues as the body of Christ is formed by the resurrected Jesus. The hands and feet of Jesus are about to go metaphorically global in the upcoming book of Acts. But for now, the presence of Jesus is recognized in his literal hands and feet.

CORE TEACHING

Ever seen a ghost?

I had heard from a reliable friend that one of my old college acquaintances had died. The deceased was a person I knew well enough to recognize instantly but not well enough to travel a few hundred miles for the funeral. My mental computer grieved the loss and placed the departed friend in its deceased file.

About a year later, I rounded the corner in Indianapolis and came face to face with the deceased. He recognized me immediately and called my name. I'm sure the look on my face must have said something other than, *Glad to see you.* We embraced.

And I said something stupid. "I thought you were dead."

Apparently not! My information had been slightly off. It's hard on your whole body to remove someone from the deceased file.

Jesus appears to the disciples. It isn't a *total* shock because reports of the dead man walking are coming from every direction. Women have been to the tomb and found no body. Cleopas and companion are gushing exuberance all over the room, still trying to catch their breath from the seven-mile sprint that began in Emmaus.

And then Jesus appears to them. He shows them his hands and feet. The risen Lord is recognized by his hands and feet. (This was long before it was common knowledge that fingerprints and footprints can't be faked because each is unique.) He showed them his hands and feet.

Our world mostly identifies people by the face. Identity cards have a picture of our face. Driver's licenses bear our face. Yearbooks display our face. Family albums capture our face. Wasn't the face of Jesus enough?

Can you imagine identifying people by their hands and feet? "Suspect has webbed toes, pinkie bent inward, chewed fingernails, noticeable crook in the pointer." We don't look at each other's hands and feet. But that's the evidence Jesus gave them. He showed them those hands that had held children, broken bread, pressed mud into blind eyes, stilled storms, pointed at fig trees, and received spikes. He showed them those feet that had walked on water, been washed by a sinner, and carried a cross to Golgotha. He showed them the hands and feet that had served us in life and death. And they knew it was him.

GOING DEEPER

The doctors told Wendy they had done all they could at the hospital and sent her home to die. Her husband, Dave, set up the hospice bed next to their queen-sized bed. She had fought the cancer for years and now had come home to die.

That first night home, Dave was sleeping in the bed next to hers and heard her stirring. She was saying, "Goodbye. Goodbye. Goodbye."

Dave said it was as if Wendy was lining up all her family and friends and bidding them farewell, one at a time. Then Wendy paused and asked of the dark night, "Jesus, are you there?"

Dave told us that this was the hardest moment in the whole ordeal—the moment when Wendy asked, and he wondered, if Jesus would be with them. He cried into his pillow and prayed. "You've got to come help me. I can't do this without you. You've got to come."

Early the next morning, people from the church began to arrive, brought there by faithful feet that knew where Jesus wanted to go. They held in their hands casseroles, hugs, cleaning supplies, back rubs, and any other deed that needed doing. And Dave's prayer was answered. Jesus had appeared. He showed Dave his hands and feet.

CONSIDER THIS

1. Why do the disciples not recognize Jesus's face? Might Luke be telling us something about the resurrection body?

2. The resurrected Jesus still bears the scars of his suffering. How does this encourage a Christian who has suffered?

3. When have you found joy in being the hands and feet of Jesus?

4. Where should these feet go this week, and what should these hands do?